Giovanni-Andrea Gallini

A Treatise on the Art of Dancing

Giovanni-Andrea Gallini

A Treatise on the Art of Dancing

ISBN/EAN: 9783742889478

Manufactured in Europe, USA, Canada, Australia, Japa

Cover: Foto ©Thomas Meinert / pixelio.de

Manufactured and distributed by brebook publishing software
(www.brebook.com)

Giovanni-Andrea Gallini

A Treatise on the Art of Dancing

A

TREATISE

ON THE

ART

OF

DANCING.

By *Giovanni-Andrea Gallini*.

L O N D O N:
Printed for the AUTHOR;
And Sold by R. DODSLEY, in *Pall-Mall*; T. BECKET
and P. A. DE HONDT, in the *Strand*; J. DIXWELL
in *St. Martin's-Lane*, near *Charing-Cross*;
A N D
At Mr. BREMNER's Mufic Shop, oppofite *Somerfet-
Houfe*, in the *Strand*.
MDCCLXXII.

THE

TABLE

OF

CONTENTS.

ADVERTISEMENT.

WHAT I have here to say is rather in the nature of an apology than of a preface or advertisement. The very title of a Treatise upon the art of dancing by a dancing-master, implicitly threatens so much either of the exageration of the profession, or of the recommendation of himself, and most probably of both, that it cannot be improper for me to

A   be-

befpeak the reader's favorable precaution againſt ſo natural a prejudice. My principal motive for hazarding this production is, indiſputably, gratitude. The approbation with which my endeavours to pleaſe in the dances of my compoſition have been honored, inſpired me with no ſentiment ſo ſtrongly as that of deſiring to prove to the public, that ſenſibility of its favor; which, in an artiſt, is more than a duty. It is even one of the means of obtaining its favor, by its inſpiring that aim at perfection,

in

in order to the deferving it, which is unknown to a merely mercenary fpirit. Under the influence of that fentiment, it occurred to me, that it might not be unpleafing to the public to have a fair ftate of the pre-tentions of this art to its en-couragement, and even to its efteem, laid before it, by a practitioner of this art. In ftating thefe pretentions, there is nothing I fhall more avoid than the enthufiafm arifing from that vanity or felf-con-ceit, which leads people into the ridicule of over-rating the

A 2   merit

merit or importance of their
profeffion. I fhall not, for example, prefume to recommend
dancing as a virtue; but I
may, without prefumption, reprefent it as one of the principal graces, and, in the juft
light, of being employed in
adorning and making Virtue
amiable, who is far from rejecting fuch affiftence. In the
view of a genteel exercife, it
ftrengthens the body; in the
view of a liberal accomplifhment, it vifibly diffufes a graceful agility through it; in the
view of a private or public en-
ter-

tertainment, it is not only a general inftinct of nature, exprefling health and joy by nothing fo ftrongly as by dancing; but is fufceptible withall of the moft elegant collateral embellifhments of tafte, from poetry, mufic, painting, and machinery.

One of the greateft and moft admired inftitutors of youth, whofe fine tafte has been allowed clear from the leaft tincture of pedantry, Quintilian recommends efpecially the talent of dancing, as conducive

to

to the formation of orators;
not, as he very juftly obferves,
that an orator fhould retain
any thing of the air of a dancing-mafter, in his motion or
gefture; but that the impreffion from the graces of that
art fhould have infenfibly
ftoln into his manner, and
fafhioned it to pleafe.

Even that auftere critic,
Scaliger, made the principles
of it fo far his concern, that
he was able perfonally to fa-
tisfy an Emperor's curiofity,
as to the nature and meaning
of

of the Pirrhic dance, by executing it before him.

All this I mention purely to obviate the prepoffeffion of the art being fo frivolous, fo unworthy of the attention of the manly and grave, as it is vulgarly, or on a fuperficial view, imagined. It is not high notions of it that I am fo weak as to aim at impreffing; all that I wifh is to give juft ones : it being perhaps as little eligible, for want of confideration, to fee lefs in this art

than

than it really deſerves, than, from a fond partiality for it, to ſee more than there is in it.

A

A

TREATISE

ON THE

ART of DANCING.

Of the ANTIENT *Dance.*

IN moſt of the nations among the
antients, dancing was not only
much practiſed, but conſtituted
not even an inconſiderable part of their
religious rites and ceremonies. The
accounts we have of the ſacred dances,
of the Jews eſpecially, as well as of
other nations, evidently atteſt it.

The

The Greeks, who probably took their firſt ideas of this art, as they did of moſt others, from Egypt, where it was in great eſteem and practice, carried it up to a very high pitch. They were in general, in their bodies, extremely well conformed, and diſpoſed for this exerciſe. Many of them piqued themſelves on rivalling, in excellence of execution, the moſt celebrated maſters of the art. That majeſtic air, ſo natural to them, while they preſerved their liberty, the delicacy of their taſte, and the cultivated agility of their limbs, all qualified them for making an agreeable figure in this kind of entertainment. Nothing could be more graceful than the motion of their arms. They did not ſo much regard the nimbleneſs and capering with the legs and feet, on which we lay ſo great a ſtreſs. Attitude,

grace,

grace, expreffion, were their principal object. They executed fcarce any thing in dancing, without fpecial regard to that expreffion which may be termed the life and foul of it.

Their fteps and motions were all diftinct, clear, and neat; proceeding from a ftrength fo fuppled, as to give their joints all the requifite flexibility and obedience to command.

They did not fo much affect the moderately comic, or half ferious, as they did the great, the pompous, or heroic ftile of dance. They fpared for no pains nor coft, towards the perfection of their dances. The figures were exquifite.. The leaft number of the figurers were forty or fifty. Their dreffes were magnificent and in tafte. Their decorations were fublime. A

competent

competent skill in the theatrical, or
actor's art, and a great one in that of
dancing, was neceffary for being admitted
into the number of figurers. In fhort,
every thing was in the higheft order,
and very fit to prove the miftake of
thofe who imagine that the dances are,
in operas for example, no more than a
kind of neceffary expletive of the intervals of the acts, for the repofe of the fingers.

The Greeks confidered dancing in
another point of light; all their feftivals
and games, which were in greater
number than in other countries, were
intermixed and heightened with dances
peculiarly compofed in honor of their
deities. From before their altars, and
from their places of worfhip, they were
foon introduced upon their theatres,
to which they were undoubtedly a prior
invention. The ftrophe, antiftrophe,
and

and epode, were nothing but certain
meafures performed by a chorus of
dancers, in harmony with the voice;
certain movements in dancing correfpondent to the fubject, which were all
along confidered as a conftitutive part
of the performance. The dancing even
governed the meafure of the ftanzas;
as the fignification of the words ftrophe
and antiftrophe, plainly imports, they
might be properly called danced himns.
The truth is, that tragedy and comedy,
made alfo originally to be fung, but
which, in procefs of time, upon truer
principles of nature, came to be acted
and declaimed, were but fuper-inductions
to the chorufes, of which, in tragedy
efpecially, the tragic-writers, could not
well get rid, as being part of the religious ceremony.

This

This folves, in a great meafure, the feeming abfurdity of their interference with the fubject of the drama : being deemed fo indifpenfable a part of the performance, that the fcene itfelf was hardly more fo : confequently, there was no fecret fuppofed to be more violated by fpeaking before them, than before the inanimate fcene itfelf. But what was at leaft excufable, on this footing, in the antients, would be an unpardonable abfurdity in the moderns.

Athenæus, who has left us an account of many of the antient dances, as the *Mactrifmus*, a dance entirely for the female fex, the *Moloffic*, the Perfian *Sicinnis*, &c. obferves, that in the earlieft ages of antiquity, dancing was efteemed an exercife, not only not inconfiftent with decency and gravity,

but

but practifed by perfons of the greateft worth and honor. Socrates himfelf, learnt the art, when he was already advanced in years.

Cautious as I am of ufing a falfe argument, I fhould fay, that the making dances a part of their religious ceremonies, was a mark of their attributing even a degree of fanctity to them; but that I am aware there were many things that found a place in their feftivals and games, which, among thofe heathens, were fo far from having any thing of facred in them, that they did not even fhow a refpect for common decency or morality.

But as to dancing, it may be prefumed, that that exercife was confidered as having nothing intrinfically in it, contrary to purity of manners or chaftity,

since

since it made a confiderable part of
the worfhip paid to the prefiding goddefs of that virtue, Diana, in the feftivals confecrated to her. Her altar was
held in the higheft veneration by the
antients. Temples of the greateft magnificence were erected in honor of this
goddefs. Who does not know the great
Diana of Ephefus ? The affemblies in
her temples were folemn, and at ftated
periods. None were admitted but
virgins of the moft fpotlefs character.
They executed dances before the altar,
in honor of the deity, with a moft
graceful decency ; invoking her continual infpiration of pure thoughts, and
her protection of their chaftity. Thofe
of them, who diftinguifhed themfelves
above the reft, by fuperior graces of
performance, received rewards not only
from the prieftefs of Diana, but from
their own parents. Nor were the young
men

men but curioufly inquifitive, as to who
particularly excelled on thefe occafions.
Diftinction in thefe dances was a great
incentive to love, and produced many
happy unions.

Such of thefe virgins as married, re-
tained, in quality of wives, fuch a veneration for this fort of worfhip, that they
formed an affembly of matrons, who
on fet days, performed much the fame
devotion, imploring, in concert, of
the goddefs, a continuance of her gifts,
and of that fpirit of purity, the fitteft to
make them edifying examples of con-
jugal love and maternal tendernefs.

Innocent amufements having been
ever reputed allowable, and even neceffary expedients for relaxing both mind

C   and

and body from the fatigue of ferious or robuft occupations, Diana
had her temples, efpecially in countries
proper for hunting, where the parents
ufed to refort with their children, and encouraged them to partake of the diverfions
in which dancing had a principal fhare.

The antients have left us an unac-
countable defcription of the Bacchanalians, whofe deportment forms a ftriking contraft to the decent regularity obferved in the worfhip of Diana.
The Bacchanalians ftrolled the country,
and, in the courfe of that vagabond
fcheme, erected temporary huts, their
refidence being always fhort wherever
they came. In their intoxication they
feemed to defy all decency and order;
affecting noife, and a kind of tumultu-
ous, boifterous joy, in which there
could never be any true pleafure or harmony.

mony. They were, in the licentiouf-
nefs of their manners, a nuifance to fo-
ciety; which they fcandalized and dif-
turbed by their riots, their mad frolics,
and even by their quarrels. Their heads
and waifts were bound with ivy, and in
their hands they brandifhed a thirfus,
or kind of lance, garnifhed with vine-
leaves. When by any foulnefs of weather they were driven into their huts,
they paffed their time in a kind of noify
merriment, of fhoutings and dithiram-
bic catches, accompanied by timpa-
nums, by cymbals, by fiftrums, and other
inftruments, in which noife was more
confulted than mufic, and correfponded
to the fort of time they kept to them,
in the frantic agitations of their Bacchic
enthufiafm. The Corybantes were called fo from their diforderly dancing as
they went along.

The

The Pirrhic dance differs not much from Plato's military dance. The invention of it is moſt generally attributed to Pirrhus, ſon of Achilles; at leaſt this opinion is countenanced by Lucian, in his treatiſe upon dancing; though it is moſt probably derived from the Memphitic dance of Egypt. The manner of it was to dance armed to the ſound of inſtruments. Xenophon takes notice of theſe dances in armour, eſpecially among the Thracians, who were ſo warlike a people. In their dance to muſic, they exhibited the imitation of a battle. They executed various evolutions; they ſeemed to wound each other mortally, ſome falling down as if they had received their death-wound; while thoſe who had given the blow ſung to the ſong of triumph, call-

ed

ed *Sitalia,* and then withdrew, leaving
the reft to take up their feeming dead
comrade, and to make preparations for
his mock-funeral, in the pantomime
ftile of dance. He has alfo defcribed
the dance of the Magnefians, in which
they reprefented their tilling the ground,
in an attitude, and in readinefs for defence, againft expected moroders. They
put themfelves in a pofture of protecting
their plough, with other motions expreffive of their refolution and courage, all
adapted to the found of the flute.
The moroders arrive, prevail, and bind
the hufbandmen to their plough, and
this terminates the dance. Sometimes
the dance varies, and the husbandmen
prevailing, bind the moroders.

The fame author mentions alfo the
Myfians who danced in armour, and
ufed a particular fort of *peltæ* or targets,

on

on which they received the blows.   In
ſhort, theſe armed dances had different
names beſtowed upon them, according
to the countries in which they were
uſed.

The Egyptians and Greeks were ex-
travagantly expenſive in their public feſtivals, of which, dancing always conſtituted a confiderable part.

The Romans, among whom the more
coarſe and licentious dances derived from
the Hetruſcans, had at firſt prevailed,
came at length to adopt the improvements of taſte, and conſequently of decency and regularity ; the feſtivals, of
which dancing was to compoſe the principal entertainment, were adapted to
the ſeafon of the year.

Every autumn, for example, it was
a conſtant cuſtom, for thoſe who could
afford

afford the expence, to build a magnificent faloon in the midft of a delightful garden. This ball-room was decorated in the moft brilliant manner: At one end of the ball-room ftood a ftatue of Pomona, furrounded with a great number of bafkets made in the neateft manner, and full of all the fineft fruits that the feafon produced. Thefe, with the ftatue, were placed under a canopy hung round with clufters of real grapes and vine-leaves, fo artfully difpofed as to appear of the natural growth. Thefe ferved to refrefh both the eye and mouth. The performers of the ball went up to this part of the faloon, in couples, proceffionally, to avoid confufion. Each youth took care to help his partner to what fhe liked beft, and then returned, in the fame regular manner, to the other end of the room, when they ferved what remained to the reft of

the

the fpectators. After which the ball immediately began.

I was fhown, by an Italian painter, a curious picture in his poffeffion, of the antients celebrating one of this kind of feftivals. The attitudes into which the figures were put, and which appeared to have been drawn for the conclu-fion of the ball, were beautiful beyond imagination.

In winter there were balls in the city of Rome; for which the appro-priated apartments were commodious; and where the illuminations were fo great, that notwithftanding the ufual rigor of that feafon, the room was fuf-ficiently warm.

Round the room there were tables and ftands, on which was placed the defert; and there were generally twelve per-fons

fons chofen to diftribute the refrefh-
ments, and do the honors of the ball.
The whole was conducted with the
utmoft decency and regularity, while
Rome preferved her refpect for virtue
and innocence of manners.

By the beft accounts procurable,
their ferious dances were properly inter-
fperfed and inlivened with comic movements. Their firft fteps were folemn
and majeftic, and, by couples they turned
under each other's arms; and when the
whole thus turned together, they could
not but afford a pleafing fight. After
which they refumed the ferious again,
and fo proceeded alternately till they
concluded the dance.

In the fpring, the country became
naturally the fcene of their dances. The
beft companies reforted, efpecially to
D   fuch

such villages as were noted for the most
pure and salubrious springs of water.
If the weather was mild, they danced
upon an open green; if not, they formed
a large covered pavilion, in the middle
of which they placed the statue of
Flora, ornamented with flowers, round
which they performed their dances.
First the youth, then those of riper years;
and lastly, those of a more advanced
age. After each of these divisions had
danced separately, they all joined and
formed one great circle. The most
distinguished for excellence in the performing these dances, had for reward the
privilege of taking a flower, with great
solemnity, from the statue of the goddess.
This was esteemed so high an honor,
that it is scarce imaginable how great an
emulation this inspired; as this privilege
was to be obtained by the impartial de-
termination of the best judges.

Sum-

Summer was however the feafon in which the pleafure of dancing was carried to the higheft pitch. For the fcene of it, they chofe a fhady and delightful part of a wood, where the funfhine could not incommode them, and where care was taken to clear the ground underfoot, for their performance. A young lady of the moft eminence for rank and beauty was chofen to perfonate the goddefs Ceres. Her drefs was of an exquifite tafte, ornamented with tufts of gold, in imitation of wheatfheaves: while her head was decked with a kind of crown compofed of fpangles, reprefenting the ears of ripe corn, and perhaps, for the greater fimplicity, of the natural grain itfelf. Thofe who danced round her, all wore wreaths of the choiceft flowers, and were drefled in white, with their hair flowing loofe, in the ftile of wood-nimphs. On this

D 2 occa-

occafion, there was always a great croud of fpectators; and the joy that appeared in each parent's eye, when their daughters were applauded, made no fmall part of the entertainment. As garlands, and wreaths of flowers compofed the principal ornament of the perfons who performed in this dance, fuch a refpect was had for it by the people in general, that they abftained from gathering any flowers, till after this feftival was over.

I have myfelf feen a drawing of this rural dance, in which I counted no lefs than fixty performers.

The celebrated Pilades is mentioned to have been the great improver of this dance. He excluded from it all jumping or capering, for fear of violating or of disfiguring the graceful regularity of

the

ART OF DANCING. 37

the whole, which he confidered as the moft effential towards preferving a pleafing effect.

Not lefs than two months were the ufual time of preparation for this dance, to which there was always a confluence of perfons from all the neighbouring parts. But none were allowed the liberty of dancing, except perfons of the firft rank and diftinction in the country; the whole being regulated by fome perfon acting in quality of *choragus*, or director of the dance.

The reign of Auguftus Cæfar was undoubtedly the epoch, of the eftablifhment in Rome, of the art of dancing in its greateft fplendor. Cahufac, an ingenious French author, in his hiftorical treatife of this art, affigns to that emperor a deep political defign in giving it

fo

ſo great an encouragement as he undoubtedly did ; that of diverting the Romans from ſerious thoughs on the loſs of
their liberty ; eſpecially in fomenting
a diſſention among them, about ſo frivolous an object as the competition between thoſe two celebrated dancers, Pilades and Bathillus. That ſomething of
this ſort might be the deſign of that emperor, is not to be doubted ; but Cahuſac,
over-heated, perhaps, by his ſubject, ex-
agerates the importance of it beyond
the bounds of cool reaſon. So much
however is true, that thoſe two dancers
were extremely eminent in their art,
and may be eſteemed the founders of
that theatrical dancing, or pantomime
execution, for which it is not ſufficient
to be only a good dancer, but there is
alſo required the being a good actor ;
in both which lights, theſe two artiſts
were allowed to excel, Pilades in the
ſerious

ferious or tragic dance, Bathillus in the comic.

Thefe alfo founded a kind of acade-mies of dancing, which produced feve-ral eminent artifts, but none that ever equalled themfelves in performance or reputation. What hiftory records of them, and of their powers, as well as of that theatrical pantomime dance, of which they were the introductors, in Rome, would exceed belief, if it was not attefted by fuch a number of au-thors as leave no room to think it an impofition.

. But as to dancing itfelf, either con-fidered in a religious, or in only an amu-five light, it may be pronounced to have been among the Romans, as old as Rome itfelf, and like that rude in its beginnings, but to have received gra-
dual

dual improvement, as faft as the other arts and fciences gained ground.

Proceffional dances were alfo much in vogue among that people. They had efpecially an anniverfary ceremony or proceffion, called, from its pre-eminence, fingly, POMPA, or the Pomp.

It was celebrated, in commemoration of a victory obtained over the Latians, the news of which was faid to have been brought by Caftor and Pollux, in perfon. This feftival, was, at firft, confecrated to Jupiter, Juno, and Minerva. But it' was afterwards made more general, and celebrated in honor of all the Gods. This proceffion was in the month of September. It began at the temple of *Jupiter Capitolinus,* proceeded to the *Forum Romanum,* from thence to the *Velabrum,* and after-

afterwards to the *Grand Circus*. You
have in Onuphrius Panvinius, the order
of this proceffion at large, of which the
directors were the chief magiftrates of
the city : the fons of the nobility lead-
ing the van. Thofe of the Equeftrian
order, whofe fathers were worth a
hundred and fifty thoufand fefterces,
followed on horfeback. It would be
here foreign from my purpofe to give
the whole defcription of this proceffion, and of thofe who compofed it.
It is fufficient to obferve, that proceffional dancing conftituted a confiderable part of it. The Pirrhic dance, executed to a martial air, called the *Pro-
celeumaticus*, employed the men of
arms. Thefe were followed by perfons who danced and leaped, in the
manner of Satirs, fome of them in the
drefs afcribed to *Silenus*, attended by
performers on inftruments adapted to

E   that

that character of dance. These made the comic part of the procession, and the persons representing Satirs, took care to divert the people by leaps, by a display of agility, and by odd uncouth attitudes, such as were in the character they had assumed. There were also in another part of the procession twelve *Salii*, or priests of Mars, so called from their making sacred dances in honor of that God, the most considerable part of their worship ; these were headed by their master or *Præsul,* the leader of the dance, a term afterwards assumed by the Christian Prelates. There were also the *Salian* virgins, besides another division of the *Salii* called *Agonenses* or *Collini.*

Nor is the processional dancing any thing surprizing; concerning that among the heathens, and even among the Hebrews,

Hebrews, they were greatly in ufe. Who does not know that David's dancing before the arch was but in confequence of its being one of the religious ceremonies on that occafion ?

The heathens ufed efpecially to form dances before their altars, and round the ftatues of their gods. The *Salü*, or priefts of Mars, whofe dances were fo framed as to give an idea of military exercife and activity, threw into their performance fteps fo expreffive and majeftic, as not only to defend their motions and geftures from any idea of levity and burlefque, which it is fo natural for the moderns to affociate with that of dancing, but even to infpire the beholders with refpect and a religious awe. The priefts chofen for this function, were always perfons of the nobleft afpect, fuitable to the dignity

E 2   of

of the facerdotal miniftry. And fo little
needs that dignity of the heathen miniftry be thought to be wounded or
violated by the act of dancing, in religious worfhip, that dances were actually
in ufe among the primitive Chriftians,
in their religious affemblies. There
was a place in their churches, efpecially
allotted for thefe confecrated dances,
upon folemn feftivals, which even gave
the name of *choir* to thofe parts of the
church now only appropriated to the
reading of the divine fervice, and to
finging. In Spain, it long remained an
eftablifhed cuftom for Chriftians to affemble in the church-porches, where,
in honor of God, they fang facred
himns, and to the tunes of them, performed dances, that were extremely
pleafing, for the decent and beautiful
fimplicity of the execution. All which
I mention purely to falve that inconfiftence,

fiftence, of the levity of dancing with the gravity of divine worſhip. An inconſiſtence of which the antients had no idea; ſince, on that occaſion, they almoſt conſtantly joined dancing to ſinging.

They are both natural expreſſions of joy and feſtivity; and as ſuch they thought neither of them improper in an addreſs of gratulation to the deity, whom they ſuppoſed rather pleaſed at ſuch innocent oblations of the heart, exulting in his manifold bounties and bleſſings.

From before the altar, among the heathens, the admiſſion of dances upon the theatre, was rather an extenſion of their power to entertain, than a total change of their deſtination; ſince the theatres themſelves were dedicated to the

the worſhip *of the heathen deities,* of
which their making a part was one of
the principal objections of the primitive Chriſtians to the theatres themſelves. However, it was from the theatres that dancing received its great and
capital improvement.

As an exerciſe, the virtue of dancing
was well known to the antients, for its
keeping up the ſtrength and agility of
the human body. There is a remark
which I ſubmit to the conſideration
of the reader, that it is not impoſſible but that the antient Romans,
who were, generally ſpeaking, low in
ſtature, and yet were eminently ſtrong,
owed that advantage to their cultivation of bodily exerciſe. This kept their
limbs ſupple, and rendered their conſtitution ſtout and hardy. Now, very la-
borious exerciſes would rather wear out
the

the machine than they would invigorate it, if there was not a due relaxation, which fhould not, however, be too abrupt a tranfition from the moft fatiguing ex-ercifes to a ftate of abfolute reft. Where-as that dancing, of which they were fo fond, afforded them, not only a pleafing employ of vacant hours, but, withall, in its keeping up the pliability of their limbs, made them find more eafe in the application of themfelves to more athletic, or to more violent exercifes, either of war or of the chace : while all together bred that firmnefs of their mufcles, that robuft compactnefs and vigor of body, which enabled them to atchieve that military valor, to which they owed all their conquefts and their glory.

Certain it is then, that among theRo-mans, even in the moft martial days of

that

that republic, the art of dancing was taught, as one of the points of accomplifhment neceffary to the education of youth ; and was even practifed among the exercifes of the Circus. I need not obferve, that there were alfo various abufes of dancing, which they very juftly accounted difhonorable to thofe who practifed them, whether in public or private. Thefe, in the degenerate days of Rome, grew to an enormous excefs. But I prefume no one will judge of an art by the abufe that may be made of it.

OF

OF

DANCING

IN GENERAL.

THIS is one of the arts, in which, as in all the reft, the ftudy of nature is efpecially to be recommended. She is an unerring guide. She gives that harmony, that power of pleafing to the productions of thofe who confult her, which fuch as neglect her muft never expect. They will furnifh nothing but monfters and difcordances; or, at the beft, but fometimes lucky hits, without meaning or connexion.

F   All

All the imitative arts acknowledge this principle.

In Poetry, a happy choice of the moſt proper words for expreſſing the ſentiments and images drawn from the obſervation of nature, conſtitutes the principal object of the poet.

In Painting, the diſpoſition of the ſubject, the reſemblance of the coloring to that of the original, in ſhort the greateſt poſſible adherence to nature, is the merit of that art.

In Muſic, that expreſſion of the paſſions which ſhould raiſe the ſame in the hearer, whether of joy, affliction, tenderneſs, or pity, can never have its effect without marking and adopting the reſpective ſounds of each paſſion as they are furniſhed by nature.

In

In Dancing, the attitudes, gestures, and motions derive also their principle from nature, whether they caracterise joy, rage, or affection, in the bodily expression respectively appropriated to the different affections of the soul. A consideration this, which clearly proves the mistake of those, who imagine the art of dancing solely confined to the legs, or even arms; whereas the expression of it should be pantomimically diffused through the whole body, the face especially included.

Monsieur Cahusac, in his ingenious treatise on this art, has very justly observed, that both singing and dancing must have existed from the primeval times; that is to say, from the first of the existence of human-kind itself.

F 2 Observe,

" Obferve, fays he, the tender chil-
" dren, from their entry into the world,
" to the moment in which their reafon
" unfolds itfelf, and you will fee that
" it is primitive nature herfelf, that
" manifefts herfelf in the found of
" their voice, in the features of their
" face, in their looks, in all their mo-
" tions. Mark their fudden palenefs,
" their quick contortions, their pierc-
" ing cries, when their foul is affected
" by a fenfation of pain. Obferve
" again, their engaging fmile, their
" fparkling eyes, their rapid motions,
" when it is moved by a fentiment of
" pleafure. You will then be clearly
" perfuaded of the principles of mu-
" fic and dancing proceeding from the
" beginning of the world down to
" us."

Certain

Certain it is, that even in children, the motions and gefture, ftrongly paint nature; and their infantine graces are not unworthy the remarks of an artift, who will be fure to find excellence in no way more obtainable than by a rational ftudy of her, where fhe is the pureft.

The cultivation of the natural graces, and a particular care to fhun all affectation, all caricature, unlefs in comic or grotefque dances, cannot be too much recommended to thofe who wifh to make any figure in this art. It is doing a great injuftice to it, to place its excellence in capers, in brilliant motions of the legs, or in the execution of difficult fteps, without meaning or fignificance, which require little more than ftrength and agility.

I

I have already obferved, that the
Greeks, who were fo famous for this
art, as indeed for moft others, which
is no wonder, fince all the arts have fo
acknowledged an affinity with each
other, ftudied efpecially grace and dignity in the execution of their dances.
That levity of capering, that nimble-
nefs of the legs, which we fo much
admire, held no rank in their opinion.
They were inconfiftent with that clearnefs of expreffion, and neatnefs of
motion, of which they principally made
a point. The great beauty of movements, or fteps, is, for every one of
them to be diftinct; not huddled and
running into one another, fo as that
one fhould begin before the precedent
one is finifhed. This fo neceffary avoid-
ance of puzzled or ambiguous motion, can only be compaffed by an attention to fignificance and juftnefs of
action.

action. This simplicity will arise from
sensibility, from being actuated by
feelings. No one has more than one
predominant actual feeling at a time;
when that is expressed clearly, the
effect is as sure as it is instantaneous.
The movement it gives, neither in-
terferes with the immediately precedent, nor the immediately following
one, though it is prepared or introduced by the one, and prepares or in-
troduces the other.

This the Greeks could the better
effectuate, from their preference of
the sublime, or serious stile; which,
having so much less of quickness or
rapidity of execution, than the comic
dance, admits of more attention to
the neat expressiveness of every motion, gesture, attitude, or step.

As

As to the great nicety of the Greeks, in the ordering and difpofing their dances, I refer to what I have before faid, for its being to be obferved, how much at prefent this art is fallen fhort of their perfection in it, and how difficult it muft be for a compofer of dances to produce them in that mafterly manner they were ufed to be performed among the antients. Let his talent for invention or compofition be never fo rich or fertile, it will be impoffible for him to do it juftice in the difplay, unlefs he is feconded by performers well verfed in the art, and efpecially expert in giving the expreffion of their part in the dance; not to mention the collateral aids of mufic, machinery, and decoration, which it is fo requifite to adapt to the fubject.

But

But where all thefe points fo neceffary are duly fupplied, and dancing is
executed in all its brilliancy, it would
be no longer looked upon, efpecially at
the Opera, as merely an expletive between the acts, juft to afford the fingers
a little breathing time. The dances
might recover their former luftre, and
give the public the fame pleafure as to
the Greeks and Romans, who made of
them one of their moft favorite entertainments, and carried them up to the
higheft pitch of tafte and excellence.

The Romans feem to have followed
the Greeks, in this paffion for dancing ;
and the theatrical dances, upon the
pantomime plan, were in Rome pufhed
to fuch a degree of perfection as is even
hard to conceive. Whole tragedies plaid,
act by act, fcene by fcene, in pantomime expreffion, give an idea of this
G   art,

art, very different from that which is
at prefent commonly received.

Every ftep in dancing has its name
and value. But not one fhould be employed in a vague unmeaning manner.
All the movements fhould be conformable to the expreffion required, and in
harmony with one another. The fteps
regular, and properly varied, with a
graceful fupplenefs in the limbs, a certain ftrength, addrefs, and agility ; juft
pofitions exhibited with eafe, delicacy,
and above all, with propriety, caracterife
the mafterly dancer, and in their union,
give to his execution its due beauty.
The leaft negligence in any of thefe
points, is immediately felt, and detracts
from the merit of the performance.
Every ftep or motion that is not natural,
or has any thing of ftiffnefs, conftraint,
or affectation, is inftinctively per-
ceived

ceived by the fpectator. The body muft
conftantly preferve its proper pofition,
without the leaft contortion, well ad-
jufted to the fteps ; while the motion
of the arms, muft be agreeable to that
of the legs, and the head to be in concert with the whole.

But in this obfervation I pretend to
no more than juft furnifhing a general
idea of the requifites towards the execution : the particulars, it is impoffible,
to give in verbal defcription, or even by
choregraphy or dances in fcore.

Many who pretend to underftand
the art of dancing, confound motions
of ftrength, with thofe of agility, mif-
taking ftrength for flight, or flight for
ftrength; tho' fo different in their nature.
It is the fpring of the body, in harmony
with fenfe, that gives the great power

G 2   to

to pleafe and furprize. The fame it is with the management of the arms; but all this requires both the theory of the art, and the practice of it. One will hardly fuffice without the other; which makes excellence in it fo rare.

The motion of the arms is as eſſential, at leaſt, as that of the legs, for an expreſſive attitude: and both receive their juſtnefs from the nature of the paſſions they are meant to exprefs. The paſſions are the fprings which muſt actuate the machine, while a clofe obſervation of nature furniſhes the art of giving to thofe motions the grace of eafe and expertnefs. Any thing that, on the ſtage efpecially, has the air of being forced, or improper, cannot fail of having a bad effect. A frivolous, affected turn of the wriſt, is furely no grace.

One

One of the moſt nice and difficult points of the art of dancing is, certainly, the management and diſplay of the arms; the adapting their motion to the character of the dance. In this many are too arbitrary in forming rules to themſelves, without conſulting nature, which would not fail of ſuggeſting to them the juſteſt movements. For want of this appropriation of geſture and attitude, the movements fit for one character are indiſtinctly employed in the repreſentation of another. And into this error thoſe will be ſure to fall, who deviate from the unerring principles of nature; which has for every character an appropriate ſtrain of motion and geſture.

Nothing then has a worſe effect, than any impropriety in the management of the arms : it gives to the eye,

the

the fame pain that difcordance in mufic does to the ear.

There are fome who move their
arms with a tolerably natural grace,
without knowing the true rules rifing
out of nature into art : but where the
advantage of theory gives yet a greater
fecurity, confequently a greater eafe
and a nobler freedom to the motions of
the performer ; the performance cannot but meet with fuller approbation.
And yet it may be as bad to fhow too
much art, as to have too little. The
point is to employ no more of art than
juft what ferves to grace nature, but
never to hide or obfcure her.

Great is the difference between the
antient and the modern dances. The
antient ones were full of fublime fimplicity. But that fimplicity was far
from

from excluding the delicate, the graceful, and even the brilliant. The .mo-
derns are fo accuftomed to thofe dances
from which nature is banifhed, and
falfe refinements fubftituted in her
room, that it is to be queftioned
whether they would relifh the return-
ing in practice to the purer principles
of the art. Myfelf knowing better,
and fenfible that the principles of nature are the only true ones, have been
fometimes forced to yield to the torrent
of fafhion, and to adopt in practice
thofe florifhings of art, which in
theory I defpifed ; and juftly, for furely the plaineft imitation of nature muft
be the grounds from which alone the
performance can be carried up to any
degree of excellence. It is with our
art, as in architecture, if the foundation is not right, the fuperftructure
will be wrong.

This

This primitive fource then muft be ftudied, known, and well attended to ; or we only follow the art blindly, and without certainty. Thence the common indifference of fo many performers, who mind nothing more than a rote of the art, without tracing it to its origin, nature.

To fucceed, we muft abandon the falfe tafte, and embrace the true; which is not only the beft guide to perfection; but when rendered familiar, by much the moft eafy and the moft delightful. It has all the advantages that truth has over falfhood.

The greater the fimplicity of fteps in a dance, the more beautiful it is ; and requires the more attention in the performer to exactnefs and delicacy; for flownefs and neatnefs being in the character

character of fimplicity, afford the fpectator both leifure and diftinctnefs for
his examination: whereas dances of in-
tricate evolutions, or quick motions, in
their confufion and hurry, allow no
clearnefs, or time for particular obfervation.

If the merit of a theatrical dancer were
to confift, as many imagine, in nothing
but in the motions of the legs, in
cutting lively or brilliant capers, in
furprizing fteps, in the agility of the
body, in vigorous fprings, in vaulting, in
a tolerable management of the arms,
and efpecially in being well acquainted
with thofe parts of the ftage where the
perfpective gives him the greateft advantage ; the art of dancing might be,
as it is generally looked upon to be, an
art eafily acquired. Whereas, for the
attaining to a juft perfection in it, there
H   are

are many other points required, but none fo much as the clofe imitation of beautiful nature ; and that efpecially in its greateft fimplicity.

Nor fhould it be imagined that the fimplicity I recommend, tends to fave the compofer of dances any trouble of invention : on the contrary, that fort of fimplicity of execution intended to produce, by means of its adherence to nature, the greateft effect, will coft him more pains, more exertion of genius, than thofe dances of which the falfe brilliants of extravagant decoration, and of mere agility without meaning or expreffion, conftitute the merit. It is with the compofition of dances, as with that of mufic, the plaineft and the moft ftriking, are ever the moft difficult to the compofer.

The

The comic, or grottefque dancers, indeed are in poffeffion of a branch of this art, in which they are difpenfed from exhibiting the ferious or pathetic; however, they may be otherwife as well acquainted with the fundamental principles of the art, as the beft mafters. But as their fuccefs depends chiefly on awakening the rifible faculty, they commonly chufe to throw their whole powers of execution into thofe motions, geftures, grimaces, and contortions, which are fitteft to give pleafure by the raifing a laugh. And certainly this has its merit; but in no other proportion to the truth of the art, which confifts in moving the nobler paffions, than as farce is to tragedy, or to genteel comedy. They are in this art of dancing, what Hemfkirk and Teniers are in that of painting.

H 2   The

The painter, can only in his draught
prefent one fingle unvaried attitude in
each perfonage that he paints : but it
is the duty of the dancer, to give, in
his own perfon, a fucceffion of attitudes,
all like thofe of the painter, taken from
nature.

Thus a painter who fhould paint
Oreftes agitated by the furies, can only
give him one fingle expreffion of his
countenance and pofture : but a dancer,
charged with the reprefentation of that
character, can, feconded by a well-
adapted mufic, execute a fucceffion of
motions and attitudes, that will more
ftrongly and furely with more livelinefs,
convey the idea of that character,
with all its tranfports of fury and
diforder.

It

It was in this light, that the antients required the union of the actor and of the dancer in the fame perfon. They expected, on the theatre efpecially, dances of character, that fhould exprefs to the eye the fenfations of the foul : without which, they confidered it as nothing but an art that had left nature behind it ; a mere corpfe without the animating fpirit ; or at the beft, carrying with it a character of falfity or tafteleffnefs. A thorough mafter of dancing, fhould, in every motion of every limb, convey fome meaning ; or rather be all expreffion or pantomime, to his very fingers ends.

How many requifites muft concur to form an accomplifhed poffeffion of this talent! It is not enough that the head fhould play on the fhoulders with all the grace of a fine connection ; nor

that

that his countenance fhould be enlivened
with fignificance and expreffion ; that
his eyes fhould give forth the juft language of the paffions belonging to the
character he reprefents ; that his
fhoulders have the eafy fall they
ought to have ; let even the motions of
his arms be true ; let his elbows and
wrifts have that delicate turn of which
the grace is fo fenfible ; let the movement of the whole perfon be free,
genteel, and eafy ; let the attitudes of
the bending turn be agreeable ; his
cheft be neither too full nor too narrow;
his fides clean made, ftrong, and well
turned ; his knees well articulated, and
fupple ; his legs neither too large, nor
too fmall, but finely formed ; his inftep furnifhed with the ftrength neceffary to execute and maintain the fprings
he makes ; his feet in juft proportion to
the fupport of the whole frame; all
thefe

thefe, accompanied with a regularity or
motion; and yet all thefe, however effential, conftitute but a fmall part of
the talent. Towards the perfection of
it, there is yet more, much more required, in that fenfibility of foul, which
has in it fo much more of the gift of
nature, than of the acquifition of art;
and is perhaps in this, what it is in moft
other arts and fciences, if not genius
itfelf, an indifpenfable foundation of
genius. There is no executing well
with the body, what is not duly felt by
the foul: fentiment gives life to the
execution, and propriety to the looks,
motions and geftures.

Thofe who would make any confiderable progrefs in this art, fhould,
above all things, ftudy juftnefs of action.
They cannot therefore too clofely at-
tend to the reprefentation of nature,
either

either upon the ſtage, or in life. I cannot too often repeat it; thoſe who keep
moſt the great original, Nature, in view,
will ever be the greateſt maſters of this
art.

As to the different characters of
dances, there are, properly ſpeaking,
four diviſions of the characters of dances:
the ſerious, the half ſerious, the comic,
and the grotteſque; but for executing
any of them with grace, the artiſt
ſhould be well grounded in the principles of the ſerious dance, which will
give him what may be called a delicacy
of manner in all the reſt.

But as one of theſe diviſions may be
more adapted to the humor, genius,
or powers of an artiſt, than another, he
ſhould, if he aims at excellence, exa-
mine carefully for which it is that he
is the moſt fit.

After

After determining which, whatever imperfections he may have from nature; he muft fet about correcting, as well as he can, by art. Nothing will hardly be found impoffible for him to fubdue, by an unfhaken refolution, and an intenfe application.

Happy indeed is that artift, in whom both the requifites of nature and art are united : but where the firft is not grofsly deficient, it may be fupplemented by the fecond. However well a beginner may be qualified for this profeffion by nature, if he does not cultivate the talent duly, he will be furpaffed by another, inferior to him in natural endowments, but who fhall have taken pains to acquire what was wanting to him, or to improve where

I   deficient.

deficient. The experience of all ages attefts this.

The helps of a lively imagination, joined to great and affiduous practice, carry the art to the higheft perfection. But practice will give no eminent diftinction without ftudy. Whoever fhall flatter himfelf with forming himfelf by practice alone, without the true principles and fufficient grounds of the art, can only proceed upon a rote of tradition, which may appear infallible to him. But this adoption of unexamined rules, and this plodding on in a beaten track, will never lead to any thing great or eminent. It carries with it always fomething of the ftiffnefs of a copy, without any thing of the graceful boldnefs of originality, or of the ftrokes of genius.

Vanity

Vanity fhould never miflead a man in the judgment he forms of his own talents : much lefs fhould an artift refort to the meannefs of depending in the fupport of cabals : it muft be the general approbation' that muft feal his patent of merit.

'I have before obferved that the grave or ferious ftile of dancing, is the great ground-work of the art. It is alfo the moft 'difficult. Firmnefs of ftep, a graceful and regular motion of all the parts, fupplenefs, eafy bendings and rifings, the whole accompanied with a good air, and managed with the greateft eafe of expertnefs and dexterity, conftitute the merit of this kind of dancing. The foul itfelf fhould be feen in every motion of the body, and exprefs fomething naturally noble, and even

heroic.

heroic. Every ſtep ſhould have its
beauty.

The painter draws, or ought to draw
his copy, the actor his action, and the
ſtatuary his model, all from the truth
of nature. They are all reſpectively
profeſſors of imitative arts; and the
dancer may well preſume to take rank
among them, ſince the imitation of
nature is not leſs his duty than theirs;
with this difference, that they have ſome
advantages of which the dancer is deſ-
titute. The Painter has time to ſettle
and correct his attitudes, but the dancer
muſt be exactly bound to the time of
the muſic. The actor has the aſſiſtance
of ſpeech, and the ſtatuary has all the
time requiſite to model his work. The
dancer's effect is not only that of a
moment, but he muſt every moment
repreſent a ſucceſſion of motions and
attitudes,

attitudes, adapted to his character, whether his fubject be heroic or paftoral, or in whatever kind of dancing he exhibits himfelf. He is by the expreffivenefs of his dumb fhow to fupplement the want of fpeech, and that with clearnefs; that whatever he aims at reprefenting may be inftantaneoufly apprehended by the fpectator, who muft not be perplexed with hammering out to himfelf the meaning of one ftep, while the dancer fhall have already begun another.

In the half-ferious ftile we obferve vigor, lightnefs, agility, brilliant fprings, with a fteadinefs and command of the body. It is the beft kind of dancing for expreffing the more general theatrical fubjects. It alfo pleafes more generally.

The

The grand pathetic of the ſerious ſtile of dancing is not what every one enters into. But all are pleaſed with a brilliant execution, in the quick motion of the legs, and the high ſprings of the body. A paſtoral dance, repreſented in all the pantomime art, will be commonly preferred to the more . ſerious ſtile, though this laſt requires doubtleſs the greateſt excellence : but it is an excellence of which few but the connoiſſeurs are judges ; who are rarely numerous enough to encourage the compoſer of dances to form them entirely in that ſtile. All that he can do is to take a great part of his attitudes from the ſerious ſtile, but to give them another turn and air in the compoſition ; that he may avoid confounding the two different ſtiles of ſerious and half-ſerious. For this laſt,

it

it is impoffible to have too much agility and brifknefs.

The comic dancer is not tied up to
the fame rules or obfervations as are
neceffary to the ferious and half ferious
ftiles. He is not fo much obliged to
ftudy what may be called nature in
high life. The rural fports, and exercifes; the geftures of various mechanics or artificers will fupply him
with ideas for the execution of char-
racters in this branch. The more his
motions, fteps, and attitudes are taken
from nature, the more they will be fure
to pleafe.

The comic dance has for object the
exciting mirth; whereas, on the contrary, the ferious ftile aims more at
foothing and captivating by the harmony and juftnefs of its movements;
by

by the grace and dignity of its steps;
by the pathos of the execution.

The comic stile, however its aim may
be laughter, requires taste, delicacy, and
invention; and that the mirth it cre-
ates should not even be without wit.
This depends not only upon the execution, but on the choice of the subje-
ject. It is not enough to value one-
self upon a close imitation of nature,
if the subject chosen for imitation is
not worth imitating, or improper to
represent; that is to say, either tri-
vial, indifferent, consequently uninte-
resting; or disgustful and unpleasing.
The one tires, the other shocks. Even
in the lowest classes of life, the com-
poser must seize only what is the fit-
test to give satisfaction; and omit
whatever can excite disagreeable ideas.
It is from the animal joy of mechanics

chanics or peafants in their ceffations from labor, or from their celebration of feftivals, that the artift will felect his matter of compofition ; not from any circumftances of unjoyous poverty or loathfome diftrefs. He muft cull the flowers of life, not prefent the roots with the foil and dirt fticking to them.

Even contrafting characters, which are fo feldom attempted on the ftage, in theatrical dances, might not have a bad effect ; whereas moft of the figures in them are fimmetrically coupled. Of the firft I once faw in Germany a ftriking inftance; an inftance that ferved to confirm that affinity between the arts which renders them fo ferviceable to one another.

K   Paffing

Paffing through the Electorate of Cologne, I obferved a number of perfons of all ages, affembled on a convenient fpot, and difpofed, in couples, in order for dancing; but fo odly paired that the moft ugly old man, had for his partner the moft beautiful and youngeft girl in the company, while, on the contrary, the moft decrepid, deformed old woman, was led by the moft handfome and vigorous youth. Inquiring the reafon of fo ftrange a groupe of figures, I was told that it was the humor of an eminent painter, who was preparing a picture for the gallery at Duffeldorp, the fubject of which was to be this contraft; and that in order to take his draught from nature, he had given a treat to this ruftic company, in the defign of exhibiting at one view, the floridnefs of youth contrafted to the weaknefs and infirmities of old age, in a moral

moral light, of expofing the impropriety of thofe matches, in which the ob-
jection of a difparity of years fhould not
be duly refpected.

I have mentioned this purely to
point out a new refource of invention,
that may throw a pleafing variety into
the compofition of dances ; and fave
them from too conftant a fimmetry,
or uniformity, either of drefs or figure,
in the pairing the dancers: by which I
am as far from meaning that that fimmetry fhould be always neglected, as
that it fhould be always obferved.

The comic dance, having then the
diverfion of the fpectator, in the way
of laughing, for its object, fhould preferve a moderately buffoon fimplicity,
and the dancer, aided by a natural genius, but efpecially by throwing as
K 2   much

much nature as poſſible into his execution, may promiſe himſelf to amuſe
and pleaſe the ſpectator; even though
he ſhould not be very deep in the
grounds of his art; provided he has a
good ear, and ſome pretty or brilliant
ſteps to vary the dance. The ſpectators
require no more.

As to the groteſque ſtile of dance, the
effect of it chiefly depends on the leaps
and height of the ſprings. There is
more of bodily ſtrength required in it
than even of agility and ſlight. It
is more calculated to ſurprize the eye,
then to entertain it. It has ſomething
of the tumbler's, or wire-dancer's merit
of difficulty and danger, rather than of
art. But the worſt of it is, that this
vigor and agility laſt no longer than the
ſeaſon of youth, or rather decreaſe in
proportion as age advances, and, by this

means

means, leave those who have trusted solely to that vigor and agility deprived of their effential merit. Whereas such as shall have joined to that vigor and agility, a proper study of the principles of their art; that talent will still remain as a resource for them. Commonly those dancers who have from nature eminently those gifts which enable them to shine in the grottesque branch, do not chuse to give themselves the trouble of going to the bottom of their art, and acquiring its perfection. Content with their bodily powers, and with the applause their performances actually do receive from the public, they look no further, and remain in ignorance of the rest of their duty. Against this diffipation then, which keeps them always superficial,
they

they cannot be too much, for their own advantage, admonifhed.

They will not otherwife get at the truth of their art, like him who qualifies himfelf for making a figure in the ferious, and half-ferious ftiles, which alfo contribute to diffufe a grace over every other kind of dancing, however different from them.

But though the grotefque may be a caricature of nature, it is never to lofe fight of it. It muft ever bear a due relation to the objects of which it attempts to exhibit the imitation, however exagerated. But in this it is for genius to direct the artift. And it is very certain that this kind of dancing, well executed, affords to the public, great entertainment in the way, if

what

what may be called broad mirth ; efpecially where the figure of the grotefque
dancer, his geftures, drefs, and the decorations, all contribute to the creation
of the laugh. He muft alfo avoid any
thing ftudied or affected in his action.
Every thing muft appear as natural as
poffible, even amidft the grimaces,
contortions, and extravagancies of the
character.

OF

O F

SUNDRY REQUISITES,

F O R

PERFECTION OF THE

A R T

O F

D A N C I N G.

I HAVE already obferved how neceffary it is that all the fteps, in
the theatrical dances, which have imitation for their object, fhould be intelligible at the firft glance of the eye.

This

This cannot be too much inculcated. The paſſions and manners of mankind, have all a different expreſſion, which cannot be preſented too plain, and too obvious. The adjuſtment of the motions to the character muſt be obſerved through every ſtile of dancing, the ſerious, the half-ſerious, the comic, and the grotefque. The various beauties of theſe different kinds of dances, all center in the propriety or truth of nature. Looks, movements, attitudes, geſtures, ſhould in the dancer, all have an appropriate meaning; ſo plainly expreſſed as to be inſtantaneouſly underſtood by the ſpectator, without giving him the trouble of unriddling them: otherwiſe, it is like talking to them in a foreign language for which an interpretor is needed.

But

But to give a fentiment, a man muft have it firft : where a pathetic fentiment is well poffeffed of the mind, the expreffion of it is diffufed over the whole body.

The theatre fhows to advantage a well proportioned dancer. A tall perfon appears the more majeftic on it ; but thofe of a middling ftature are more generally fit for every character ; and may make up in gracefulnefs what they want in fize. The remarkably tall commonly want the graces to be feen in thofe of the more general ftandard.

A young dancer who difplays a dawn of genius, cannot be too much exhorted to deliver himfelf up to the power of nature ; fo that acquiring a particular manner of his own, he may himfelf proceed on original. If he would hope

L 2

to

to arrive at any eminence in the art, he muft break the fhackles of a fervile imitation, and preferve nothing but the principles and grounds of his art, which will be fo far from fettering him, that they will affift his foaring upon the wings of his own genius.

Where a dancer undertakes to repre- fent a fubject on the theatre, he muft ground his plan of performance on the felecting all the moft proper fituations for furnifhing the moft ftrikingly pic- tures, profpects, and confequently, pro- ducing the greateft effect.

This was doubtlefs the great fecret of Pilades, the founder, at leaft in Rome, of the pantomime art. It was on this choice of fituations, that the under-

underftanding whole pieces, both tragic and comic, executed in dances, entirely depends.

And here, upon mentioning the pantomime art, be it allowed me to defend it againft the objections made to it, by thofe who confider it only under a partial or vulgar point of view.

If any one fhould pretend that the pantomime art is fuperior to the actor's power of reprefentation in tragedy or comedy, or that fuch an entertainment of dumb fhow ought to exclude that of fpeaking characters; nothing could be more ridiculous or abfurd than fuch a propofition.

That indeed would be rejecting one of the moft noble improvements of nature, in favor of an art rather calculated

culated for the relaxation of the mind
than for the inftruction of it ; in which
it can only claim a fubordinate fhare.

Thofe fubjects, whether ferious or
comic, which are executed by dances,
or in the pantomime ftrain, arc chiefly
intended for the throwing a variety into theatrical entertainments, without
difputing any honors of rank.

The very fame perfon who fhall
have at one time, taken pleafure in feeing and hearing the noble and pathetic
fentiments of tragedy, or the ridicule
of human follies in a good comedy,
finely reprefented, may, without any
fort of inconfiftence, not be difpleafed
at feeing, at another time, a fubject
executed in dances, while the mufic,
the decorations, all contribute to the
happy diverfification of his entertainment.

ment. Ought he therefore either to
call his own taſte to an account for his
being pleaſed, or to grudge to others a
pleaſure, which nature itſelf juſtifies,
in his having given to mankind a love
of variety?

Nor is there perhaps, in the world,
an art more the genuine offspring of
Nature, more under her immediate
command, than the art of dancing.
For to ſay nothing of that dancing,
which has no relation to the theatre,
and which is her principal demonſtra-
tions of joy and feſtivity, the theatrical
branch acknowledges her for its great
and capital guide. All the motions, all
the geſtures, all the attitudes, all the
looks, can have no merit, but in their
faithful imitation of Nature: while man
himſelf, man, the nobleſt of her productions, is ever the ſubject which the
dancer

dancer paints through all his paſſions and manners.

The painter preſents man in one fixed attitude, with no more of life than the draught and colors can give to his figure: the dancer exhibits him in a ſucceſſion of attitudes, and, inſtead of painting with the bruſh, paints, ſurely more to the life, with his own perſon. A dance in action, is not only a moving picture, but an animated one : while to the eloquence of the tongue, it ſubſtitutes that of the whole body.

The art, viewed in this light, ſhows how comparatively little the merely mechanical part of it, the agility of the legs and body, contributes to the accompliſhment of the dancer; however neceſſary that alſo is. We might ſoon form a dancer, if the art conſiſted only in his being taught

to fhake his legs in cadence, to bal-
lance his body, or to move his arms un-
meaningly. But if he has not a genius,
fufceptible of cultivation, and which is
itfelf far the moft effential gift, he will
make no progrefs towards the defirable
diftinction : he is a body without a foul:
his performance will have more of the
poppet moved by wires, than of the
actor giving that life to the character,
which himfelf receives from the fenfibility of genius.

There are many young beginners,
who, looking on this art as a good way
of livelihood, enter on the rudiments
of it, with great ardor. But this
ardor foon abates, in proportion, as
they advance, and find there is more
ftudy and pains required from them
than they expected to find, towards
their arrival at any tolerable degree of
M   perfection.

perfection. Having confidered this art
as purely a mechanical one, they are
furprifed at the difcovery of its exacting
thought and reflection, for which
their ideas of it had not prepared them.
A man who has not fufficient fhare of
genius to attempt the vanquifhing thefe
difficulties, of which, in his falfe conception of things, he has formed to himfelf no notion ; either treats thefe great
effentials of the art, as innovations, and
fuch as he is not bound to admit, or in
the defpair of acquiring them, fits
down contented with his mediocrity.
It is well if he does not rail at, or attempt to turn into ridicule, perfections
which are beyond his reach. And to
fay the truth, the art has not greater
enemies than thofe profeffors of it, who
ftick at the furface, and want the fpirit
neceffary to go to the bottom of it. In
vain does the public refufe its applaufe
to

to their indifferent, ordinary, uninterest-
ing performance : rather than allow
the fault to be in themselves, their
vanity will lay it on the public : they
never refuse themselves that approbation which others can see no reason
for bestowing on them. They are perfectly satisfied with having executed in
their little manner, the little they know
or are capable of; they have no idea of
any thing beyond their short reach.

Certainly the best season of life,
for the study of this art, is, as for that
of most others, for obvious reasons, the
time of one's youth. It is the best
time of laying the foundation both of
theory and practice.

But the theory should especially be
attended to, without however neglect-
ing the practice. For though a dancer, by an assiduous practice, may, at

the

the firſt unexamining glance, appear as
well in the eyes of the public, as he
who poſſeſſes the rules; the illuſion
will not be laſting; it will ſoon be
diſſipated, eſpecially where there is
preſent an object of compariſon. He
whoſe motions are dirrected only by rote
and cuſtom, will ſoon be diſcovered
eſſentially inferior to him whoſe practice
is governed by a knowledge of the
principles of his art.

   A maſter does not do his duty by
his pupil, in this art, if he fails of
ſtrongly inculcating to him the neceſſity
of ſtudying thoſe principles; and of
kindling in him that ardor for attaining to excellence, which if it is not
itſelf genius, it is certain that no genius
will do much without it. •

                              Invention

Invention is alfo as much a requifite in our art as in any other. But to fave the pains of ftudy, we often borrow and copy from one another. Indolence is the bane of our art. The trouble of thinking neceffary to the invention and compofition of dances, appears to many too great a fatigue : this engages them to appropriate to themfelves the fruits of other peoples invention ; and they appear to themfelves well provided at a fmall expence, when they have made free with the productions of others. Some again, inftead of cultivating their talent, chufe indolently to follow the great torrent of the fafhion, and ftick to the old tracks, without daring to ftrike out any thing new, fo that their prejudices are, in fact, the principles by which they are governed, and which fometimes ferves them for their excufe; fince they know

better,

better, but do not care to give themfelves
the trouble of acting up to their knowledge. Thus they plod on in the fafe,
and broad road of mediocrity, but
without any reputation or name. They
are neither envied nor applauded.

As for thofe who borrow from
others, content with being copies,
when they ought to ftrive to be originals ; nothing can more obftruct their
progrefs in the difcoveries of the depths
of their art, than this fcheme of fubfifting on the merit of others.

Many, befides thofe who are incapable of invention, are tempted at
once by their indolence, and by the
hope of not being difcovered or
minded in their borrowing from others,
to give ftale or hackneyed compofitions,
which having feen in one country, they
flatter

flatter themfelves they may palm for new and original upon the public in another. Thence it is that the audience is cloyed with repetitions of panto-mime dances ; perhaps fome of them very pretty at their firft appearance, but which cannot fail of tiring when too often repeated; or when the fame grounds or fubject of action is only fu-perficially or flightly diverfified.

It is this barrennefs of invention that the ingenious Goldoni has fo well ex-pofed in one of his plays, in the following fpeech, addreffed to a young man.

" * For example, you, as the female dancer;

---

* Per efempio vendra fora la ballerina, colla rocca, filando, ò con un fecchio à

" dancer will come upon the ſtage,
" with a diſtaff, twirling it, or with a
" a pail to draw water ; or with a
spade

---

trar l'acqua, ò con una zappa à zappar.
El voſtro compagno vendra fora ò colla
cariola à portar qualche coſa, ò colla falce
à tagliar il grano, ò colla pipa a fumar,
e ſi ben, che la ſcena foſſe una ſala, tanto
e tanto, ſe vien a far da contadini ò da
marinari. El voſtro compagno non vi ve-
dra : voi andarete a cercarlo, e el vi ſcac-
ciera via. Gli batterete una man ſu la
ſpalla, ed el con un ſalto anderà dall'altra
banda. Voigli correrete dietro, lui ſe
ſcampera, e voi anderete in collera.
Quando voi ſarete in collera, a lui le vendra la voglia di far pace, e lui vi pre-
ghera, voi lo ſcacciarete. Scamparete
via, e lui vi correra dietro. El ſe ingin-
occhiera, farete pace, voi, menando I pe-
dini, l'invitarete a ballar : anche ello,
menando I piedi, a ſegni dira, " balliamo,"
e tirandovi indietro allegramente comincia-

" ſpade for digging. Your companion
" will come next perhaps driving a
" wheel-barrow, or with a ſickle to mow
" corn, or with a pipe a-ſmoaking ; and
" though the ſcene ſhould be a ſaloon,
" no matter, it will come ſoon to be
       N   " filled

---

rete el *Pas-de-deux*. La prima parte alle-
gra, la ſegonda grave, la terza una giga.
Procurarete di cacciargli dentro ſei o ſette
delle migliori arie di ballo che ſ'abbiano ſen-
tito; farete tutti i paſſi che ſapete fare, e che
ſia il *Pas-de-deux* o da paeſana, o da giar-
dinera, o da Granatiera, o da ſtatue, i
paſſi ſaranno ſempre gli iſteſſi, correrſe dietro, ſcampar, pianger, andar in collera,
far pace, tirar i bracci ſopra la teſta, ſaltar
in tempo e fora di tempo, menar gli
bracci, e le gambe, e la teſta, e la vita,
e le ſpalle, e ſopra tutto rider ſempre col
popolo, e ſtorcer un pochetto il collo
quando ſi paſſa proſſimo i lumi, e fare
delle belle ſmorfie all udienza, e una bella
riverenza in ultima.

" filled with ruftics or failors. Your
" companion to be fure will not have
" feen you, at firft ; that is the rule ;
" upon which you will make up to him,
" and he will fend you a packing. You
" will tap him on the fhoulder with one
" hand, and he will give a fpring from you
" to the other fide of the ftage. You will
" run after him ; he, on his part will
" fcamper away from you, and you
" will take pet at it. When he fees
" you angry, he will take it into his
" head to make peace; he will fue
" to you, and you in your turn will
" fend him about his bufinefs. You
" will run from him, and he after
" you. He will be down on his knees
" to you; peace will be made ; then,
" fhaking your footfies, you will invite
" him to dance. He alfo will anfwer
" you with his feet, as much as to fay,
" come, let us dance."

" There

" Then handing you backwards to
" the top of the ftage, you will begin
" gaily a *Pas-de-deux*, or Duet dance.
" The firft part will be lively, the fe-
" cond grave, the third a jig. You will
" have taken care to procure fix or feven
" of the beft airs for a dance, put to-
" gether, that can be imagined. You'
" will execute all the fteps that you are
" miftrefs of ; and let your character in
" the Pas-de-deux, be that of a country
" wench, a gardener's fervant, a grana-
" dier's trull, or a ftatue ; the fteps
" will be always the fame ; and the
" fame actions for ever repeated ; fuch
" as running after one another, dodg-
" ing, crying, falling in a paffion,
" making peace again, bringing the
" arms over the head, jumping in and
" out of time, fhaking legs and arms,
" the head, the body, the fhoulders,
" and efpecially fmirking and ogling
N 2	" round

" round you ; not forgetting gentle in-
" flexions of the neck, as you pals close
" under the lights, nor to make pretty
" faces to the audience, and then, hey
" for a fine curtefy at the end of the
" dance !"

Nothing however would more obftruct the progrefs of this art, than thus
contenting one felf with adopting
the productions of others. It even
would, in the difguft which repetition occafions, bring on the decline
of this entertainment, in the opinion
of a public which is always fond of
novelty.

And of novelty, the beauties of nature furnifh an inexhauftible fund,
in their infinite variety. Among thefe
it is the bufinefs of the artift to
chufe fuch as can be brought upon
the

the fcene, and theatrically adapted to the execution of his art. But for this he muft be poffeffed of tafte, which is a qualification as neceffary to him, as a compofer, as that of the graces are to him as a performer. Both are gifts. But if a due exercife of the art can add to the natural graces, tafte does not ftand lefs in need of cultivation: it refines itfelf by a judicious obfervation of the beauties and delicacies of nature. Thefe he muft inceffantly ftudy, in order to tranfplant into his art fuch as are capable of producing the moft pleafing effect. He muft particularly confult the fitnefs of time, place and manners; otherwife what would pleafe in one dance might difpleafe in another. Propriety is the great rule of this art, as of all others. A difcordance in mufic hurts a nice ear; a falfe attitude or motion in dancing equally offends the judicious eye. The

The looks of the dancer are far from infignificant to the character he is reprefenting. Their expreffion fhould be ftrictly conformable to his fubject. The eye efpecially fhould fpeak. Thence it is that the Italian cuftom of dancing with uncovered faces, cannot but be more advantageous than that of dancing mafked, as is commonly done in France ; when the paffions can never be fo well reprefented as by the changes of expreffion, which the dancer fhould throw into his countenance.

And it is by thefe changes of countenance, as well as of attitude and gefture, that the dancer can exprefs the gradations of the paffions ; whereas the painter is confined intirely to one paffion, that of the particular moment in which he will have chofen to draw a character. For example, a painter, who means to reprefent a country-maid, under the influence of the paffion of love, can only aim at expreffing fome particular degree of that paffion, fuitable to the circumftances of the reft of his picture, or to the fituation in which he fhall have placed her. But a dancer may fucceffively reprefent all the gradations of love ; fuch as furprize at firft fight, admiration, timidity, perplexity, agitation, languor, defire, ardor, eagernefs, impatience, tumultous tranfports, with all the external fimptoms of that paffion. All thefe may be executed in the moft lively manner, in time and cadence, to a correfpondent mufic or fimphany. And fo of all the other paffions, whether of fear, revenge, joy, hatred, which have all their fubdivifions expreffible, by the quick fhift and fucceffion

ceffion of fteps, geftures, attitudes, and looks, refpectively adapted to each gradation.

A maſk then cannot but hide a great part of the neceffary expreffion, or juftnefs of action. It can only be favorable to thofe who have contracted ill habits of grimacing or of contortions of the face while they perform.

There are however fome characters in which a maſk is even neceffary : but then great care fhould be taken to model and fit it as exactly as poffible to the face, as well as to have it perfectly natural to the character reprefented. The French are particularly, and not without reafon, curious in this point.

The

The female dancers have naturally a greater eafe of expreffion than the men. More pliable in their limbs, with more fenfibility in the delicacy of their frame; all their motions and actions are more tenderly pathetic, more interefting than in our fex. We are befides prepoffeffed in their favor, and lefs difpofed to remark or cavil at their faults. While on the other hand, that fo natural defire they have of pleafing, independently of their profeffion, makes them ftudioufly avoid any motion or gefture that might be difagreeable, and confequently any contortion of the face. They, inftinctively then, one may fay, make a point of the moft graceful expreffion.

A woman, who fhould only depend on the exertion of ftrength in her legs or limbs, without attention to ex-

O   preffion,

preffion, would poffefs but a very de-
fective talent. Such an one might furprize the public, by the mafculine vigor
of her fprings; but fhould fhe attempt
to execute a dance, where tender expreffions are requifite, fhe would certainly fail of pleafing.

The female dancers have alfo an advantage over the men, in that the pet-
ticoat can conceal many defects in their
execution; even, if the indulgence
due to that amiable fex, did not only
make great allowances, but give to the
leaft agreeable fteps in them, the power
of obtaining applaufe.

At the Italian theatres at Rome, in
the Carnaval, where the female dancers
are not fuffered to perform the dances,
and where the parts of the women are perform'd by men in the dreffes of women,

it

it appears plainly, how much the execution suffers by this expedient. However well they may be difguifed, there is an inherent clumfinefs in them, which it is impoffible for them to fhake off, fo as to reprefent with juftnefs the fprightly graces and delicacy of the female fex. The very idea of feeing men effeminated by fuch a drefs, invincibly difgufts. An effeminate man appears even worfe than a mafculine woman.

But however the confulting a looking-glafs gives to men, in general, the air of fops or coxcombs; it is to thofe who would make a figure in dancing a point of neceffity. A glafs is to them, what reflexion is to a thinking perfon; it ferves to make them acquainted with their defects, and to correct them. To practice then before it is even recom-

O 2   mendable,

mendable, that practice will give the advantage of expertnefs, and expertnefs will give the grace of eafe, which is invaluable; nothing being fuch an enemy to the graces as ftiffnefs or affectation. This is a general rule both for compofition and performance.

Education has doubtlefs a great fhare in giving early to the body a command of graceful pofitions, efpecially for the grand and ferious dances, which, as I have before obferved, are the principal grounds of the art. And once more, the great point is not to stick at mediocrity; but to aim at an excellence in the art, that may give at leaft the beft chance for not being confounded with the croud. If it is true, that, among the talents, thofe which are calculated for pleafing, are not

thofe

thofe that are the leaft fure of encouragement ; it is alfo equally true, that for
any dependence to be had on them,
it is fomething more than an ordinary
degree of merit in them that is required.

In fupport of this admonition, I am
here tempted to enliven this effay with
the narrative of an adventure in real
life, that may ferve to break the too
long a line of an attempt at inftruction.

A celebrated female dancer in Italy,
defigning to perform at a certain capital,
wrote to her correfpondent there to
provide her an apartment fuitable to the
genteel figure which fhe had always made
in life. On her arrival, her acquaintance
feeing fhe had brought nothing with
her, but her own perfon and two fer-
                                    vants,

vants, afked her when fhe expected her baggage. She anfwered, with a fmile, " If you will come to-morrow morn- " ing and breakfaft with me, you, and " whoever you will bring with you, " fhall fee it, and I promife you it is " worth your while feeing, being a " fort of merchandize that is very much " in fafhion."

Curiofity carried a number early to the rendezvous, where, after an elegant breakfaft, fhe got up, and danc- ed before them in a moft furprizingly charming manner.

" Thefe, faid fhe, (pointing at her " legs,) are all the baggage I have left ; " the Alps have fwallowed up all the " reft." The truth was, fhe had been really robbed of her baggage in her journey, and the merchandize on which fhe

fhe now depended, was her talent at dancing. Nor was fhe deceived, for her inimitable performance, joined to the vivacity with which fhe bore her misfortunes, in the fpirit of the old Philofopher, who valued himfelf upon carrying his all about him, made her many friends, whofe - generous compaffion foon enabled her to appear in her former ftate.

As to the compofition of dances, it is impoffible for a profeffor of this art, to make any figure without a competent ftock of original ideas, reducible into practice.   A dance fhould be a kind of regular dramatic poem to be executed by dancing, in a manner fo clear, as to give to the underftanding of the fpectator, no trouble in making out the meaning of the whole, or of any part of it.   All

ambiguity

ambiguity being as great a fault of
ftile in fuch compofitions, as in writ-
ing. It is even harder to be repaired;
for a falfe expreffion in the motions,
geftures, or looks, may confufe and be-
wilder the fpectator fo as that he will
not eafily recover the clue or thread
of the fable intended to be reprefented.

Clearnefs then is one of the principal points of merit which the compofer fhould have in view; if the
effect, refulting from the choice and
difpofition of the ground-work of his
drama, does honor to his inventivenefs
or tafte; the juftnefs, with which every
character is to be performed, is not lefs
effential to the fuccefs of his production, when carried into execution.

To be well affured of this, it cannot but be neceffary that the compofer

pofer of the dance or ballet-mafter,
fhould be himfelf a good performer, or
at leaft underftand the grounds of
his art.

He muft alfo, in his compofition,
be pre-affured of all the neceffaries
for their complete execution. Otherwife decorations either deficient or not
well adapted; an infufficient number of
performers, or their being bad ones;
or, in fhort, the fault of a manager,
who, through a mifplaced economy,
would not allow the requifite ex-
pences; all thefe, or any of thefe,
might ruin the compofition, and the
compofer might, after taking all imaginable pains to pleafe, find his labor abortive, and himfelf condemned
for what he could not help. There
is no exhibiting with fuccefs any entertainment of this fort without hav-

P in

ing all the neceffary performers and accompaniments. It will be in a great meafure perfect or imperfect in proportion as they are fupplied or withheld.

A good ballet-mafter muft efpecially have regard to both poetical and picturefque invention; his aim being to unite both thofe arts under one exhibition. The poetical part of the compofition being neceffary to furnifh a well-compofed piece that fhall begin with a clear expofition, and proceed unfolding itfelf to the conclufion, in fituations well chofen, and well expreffed. The picturefque part is alfo highly effential for the formation of the fteps, attitudes, geftures, looks, grouping the performers, and planning their evolutions; all for the greateft and jufteft effect.

He

He fhould himfelf be thoroughly ftruck with his initial idea, which will lead him to the fecond, and fo on methodically until the whole is concluded, without having recourfe to a method juftly exploded by the beft mafters, that of choregraphy or noting dances, which only ferves to obftruct and infrigidate the fire of compofition. When he fhall have finifhed his compofition, he may then coolly review it, and make what difpofition and arrangement of the parts fhall appear the beft to him. Every interruption is to be avoided, in thofe moments, when the imagination is at its higheft pitch of inventing and projecting. There are few artifts who have not, at times, experienced in themfelves a more than ordinary difpofition or aptitude, for this operation of the mind; and it is thefe critical mo-

P 2   ments,

ments, which may otherwise be ir-
retrievable, they ought particularly to
improve, with as little diverfion from
them as poffible. They fhould pur-
fue a thought, or a hint of a thought,
from its firft crudity to its utmoft
maturity.

A man of true genius in any of
the imitative arts, and there is not
one that has a jufter claim to that
title than the art of dancing, fenfible that nature is the varied and abun-
dant fpring of all objects of imitation,
confiders her and all her effects with
a far different eye from thofe who
have no intention of availing themfelves of the matter fhe furnifhes for
obfervation. He will difcover effential differences between objects, where
a fuperficial beholder fees nothing but
famenefs; and in his imitation he
will

will fo well know how to render thofe differences difcernible, that in the compofition of his dance, the moft trite fubject will affume the air of novelty with the grace of variety.

There is nothing difgufts fo much as repetitions of the fame thing; and a compofer of dances will avoid them as ftudioufly as painters do in their pieces, or writers tautology.

The public complains, with great reafon, that dances are frequently void of action, which is the fault of the performers not giving themfelves the trouble to ftudy juft ones : fatisfied with the more mechanical part of dancing, they never think of connecting the part of the actor with it, which however is indifpenfably neceffary

ceſſary to give to their performance,
ſpirit, and animation.

A dance without meaning is a very
inſipid botch. The ſubject of the
compoſition ſhould always be ſtrictly
connected to the dances, ſo as that
they ſhould be in equal correſpon-
dence to one another. And, where a
dance is expletively introduced in the
intervals of the acts, the ſubject of
it ſhould have, at leaſt, ſome affinity
to the piece. A long cuſtom has
made the want of this attention paſs
unnoticed. It is ſurely an abſurd and
an unnatural patchwork, between the
acts of a deep tragedy, to bring on,
abruptly by way of diverſion, a comic
dance. By this contraſt both entertainments are hurt; the abruptneſs
of the tranſition is intolerable to the
audience ; and the thread, eſpecially

of

of the tragic fable, is unpleafingly broken. The fpectators cannot bear to be fo fuddenly toffed from the ferious to the mirthful, and from the mirthful to the ferious. In fhort, fuch an heterogeneous adulteration has all the abfurdity reproached to the motley mixture in tragi-comedy, without any thing of that connection which is preferved in that kind of juftly exploded dramatic compofition. How eafy too to avoid this defect, by adapting the fubjects of the dances to the different exigences of the different dramas, whether ferious, comic, or ·farcical !

One great fource of this diforder, is probably the managers confidering dances in nothing better than in the light of merely a mechanical execution for the amufement of the eye, and

and incapable of fpeaking to the mind.
And in this miftake they are certainly juftifiable by the great dege-
neracy of this art, from the pitch of
perfection to which it was antiently
carried, and to which the encouragement of the public could not fail
to reftore it. The managers would
then fee their intereft too clearly in
confulting the greater pleafure of the
public, not to afford to this art, the
requifite cultivation and means of improvement.

The compofer, who muft even have
fomething of the poet in him ; the mu-
fician, the painter, the mechanic, are
effentially neceffary to the contribution
of their refpective arts, towards the
harmony and perfection of compofition, in a fine dramatic dance ; even
the dreffes are no inconfiderable part of
the

the entertainment. The *coftume*, or in a more general term, propriety, fhould have the direction of them. It is not magnificence, that is the great point, but their being well afforted to character and circumftances. The French are notorioufly faulty in over-dreffing their characters, and in making them. fine and fhowy, where their fimplicity would be their greateft ornament. I do not mean a fimplicity that fhould have any thing mean, low or indifferent in it; but, for example, in rural characters, the fimplicity of nature, if I may ufe the expreffion, in her holyday-cloaths.

As to the decorations and machines efpecially, I know of no place where there is lefs excufe for their being deficient in them than in London, where they are too manifeftly, to bear

Q any

any fufpicion of flattery in the attributing it to them, executed to a perfection that is not known in any other part of Europe. The quicknefs with which the fhifts and deceptions in the pantomime entertainments are performed here, have been attempted in many other parts; but the perfons there employed, not having the fame fkill and depth in mechanics as the artifts here, cannot come up to them in this point. And it is in this point precifely that a compofer of dances may be furnifhed with great affiftence in the effects from the theatrical illufion. And in an entertainment, where by an eftablifhed tacit agreement between the audience and performers, there is fuch a latitude of introducing fuperhuman perfonages, either of the heathen deities, or of fairy-hood, inchanters, and the like, thofe transformations and deceptions

tions of the fight are even in the order of natural confequences, from the pre-fuppofed and allowed power of fuch characters to operate them. At the fame time the rules of probability muft even there be obferved. Nor is it amifs to be very fparing and referved in the compofition of thofe dances, grounded on the introduction of purely imaginary beings, fuch as the allegorical imperfonation of the moral Beings, whether the Virtues or the Vices. Unlefs the invention is very interefting indeed, the characters diftinctly marked, and the application very juft and obvious; their effect is rarely anfwerable to expectation, efpecially on the audiences of this country. The tafte here for thofe airy ideal characters is not very high, and perhaps not the worfe for not being fo.

Among

Among the many loffes which this art has fuftained, one furely, not the leaft regrettable, even for our theatres, was that of the dances in armour, practifed by the Greeks, which they ufed by way of diverfion and of *exercife* for invigorating their bodies. Sometimes they had only bucklers and javelins in their hands : but, on certain occafions they performed in panoply, or complete fuits of armour. Strengthened by their daily and various manly exercifes, they were enabled to execute thefe dances, with a furprifing exactnefs and dexterity. The martial fimphony that accompanied them, was performed by a numerous band of mufic; for the clafh of their arms being fo loud, would elfe have drowned the tune or airs of the muficians. It is impoffible to imagine

a more

a more fublime, fplendid and picturefque fight than what thefe dances
afforded, in the brilliancy of their arms,
and the variety of their evolutions; while
the delight they took in it, infpired
them with as much martial fire, as if
they had been actually going to meet the
enemy.. And indeed this diverfion was
fo much of the nature of the military
exercife, that none could be admitted
who were not thoroughly expert in all
martial training.   In time of peace, this
kind of dance was confidered as even
neceffary to keep up that fupplenefs and
athletic difpofition of body, to bear action and fatigue, effential to the military profeffion. If the practice had
been. neglected, but for a few days,
they obferved a numbnefs infenfibly
diffufe itfelf over the whole body.
They were perfuaded then that the
beft way of preferving their health, and
                                fitnefs

fitnefs for action, and confequently to qualify them for the moft heroic enter-prizes, was to keep up this kind of exercife, in the form of diverfion.

Thefe martial dances, have, in fome operas of Italy, been attempted to be imitated, with fome degree of fuccefs : but as the performers had not been trained up to fuch an exercife, like the Greeks, it was not to be expected that the reprefentation fhould have the fame perfection, or color of life.

The compofition of the mufic, and the fuiting the airs to the intended execution of a dance, is a point of which it is fcarce needful to infift on the importance, from its being fo ob-vious and fo well known. Nothing can produce a more difagreeable difcor-dance than a performer's dancing out
of

of time. And here it may be obferved, how much lies upon a dancer, in his being at once obliged to adapt his motions exactly to the mufic and to the character : which forms a double incumbence, neither point of which he can neglect, without falling into unpardonable errors.

Where dances are well compofed, they may give a picture, to the life, of the manners and genius of each nation and each age, in conformity to the fubject refpectively chofen. But then the truth of the *coftume*, and of natural and hiftorical reprefentation muft be ftrictly preferved. Objects muft be neither exagerated beyond probability, nor diminifhed fo as not to pleafe or affect. A real genius will not be affraid of ftriking out of the common paths, and, fen-

fible

fible that inventivenefs is a merit, he will create new theatrical fubjects, or produce varied combinations of old ones. And where the decorations, or requifite accompaniments are not fupplied as he could wifh, he muft endeavour to make the moft of what he can get, towards the exhibition of his production; if not with all the advantage of which it is fufceptible, at leaft with all thofe he can procure for it. Where the beft cannot be obtained, he muft be content with the leaft bad. But efpecially a compofer of dances fhould never lofe fight of his duty in preferving to his art its power of competition, as well as its affinity with the other imitative arts, in the expreffion of nature; all the paffions and fentiments being manifeftly to be marked by motion, geftures, and attitudes, to the time of

a

a correfpondent and well adapted mufic. While all this aided and fet off, by
the accompaniments of proper decorations of painting, and, where neceffary, of
machinery, makes that, a well compofed dance, may very juftly be deemed a fmall poem, thrown into the
moft lively action imaginable; into an
action fo expreffive as not to need
the aid of words, for conveying its
meaning; but to make the want of
them rather a pleafure than matter
of regret; from its exercifing, without fatiguing, the mind of the fpectator, to which it can never be but
an agreeable entertainment, to have
fomething left for its own making
out, always provided that there be
no perplexing difficulty or ambiguity.
Nothing of which is impoffible to an
artift who has the talent of making

R a

a right choice among the moſt pleaſing objects of nature; of ſufficiently
feeling what he aims at expreſſing;
of knowing how far it is allowable
for his art, to proceed towards the em-
belliſhing nature, and where it ſhould
ſtop to avoid its becoming an im-
pertinence; and eſpecially of agreeably diſpoſing his ſubject, in the moſt
neat and intelligible manner that can
be deſired.

SOME

SOME

THOUGHTS

On the UTILITY of

LEARNING to DANCE,

And Efpecially upon the

MINUET.

WAS I, in quality of a danc-ing-mafter, to offer even the ftrongeft reafons of inducement to learn this art, they could not but juftly lofe much, if not all, of their weight, from my fuppofed intereft in the of-

R 2   fering

fering them ; befides the partiality
every artift has for his art.

It would however exceed the bounds
prefcribed to modefty itfelf, were I to
neglect availing myfelf of the authority of others, who were not only
far from being profeffors of this art,
but who hold the higheft rank in the
public opinion for folidity of underftanding, and purity of morals, and who yet
did not difdain to give their opinion in
favor of an art only imagined frivolous,
for want of confidering it in a juft and
inlarged view.

After this introduction, I need not
be afhamed of quoting Mr. Locke,
in his judicious treatife of education.

" Nothing (fays he) appears to me
" to give children fo much becom-
" in g confidence and behaviour, and
" fo to raife them to the converfa-
" tion

" tion of thofe above their age, as danc-
" ing.   I think they fhould be taught
" to dance as foon as they are capable
" of learning it ; for though this con-
" fifts only in outward gracefulnefs of
" motion, yet, I know not how, it
" gives children manly thoughts and
" carriage more than any thing.".

In another place, he fays,

" Dancing being that which gives
" graceful motions to all our lives, and
" above all things, manlinefs, and a
" becoming confidence to young chil-
" dren, I think it cannot be learned
" too early, after they are once capable
" of it. But you muft be fure to have
" a good mafter, that knows and can
" teach what is graceful and becom-
" ing, and what gives a freedom and
" eafinefs to all the motions of the
                                    " body.

" body. One that teaches not this, is
" worfe than none at all; natural awk-
" wardnefs being much better than apifh
" affected poftures: and I think it
" much more paffable, to put off the
" hat, and make a leg like an honeft
" country-gentleman, than like an ill-
" fafhioned dancing-mafter. For as
" for the jigging, and the figures of
" dance, I count that little or nothing
" better than as it tends to perfect grace-
" ful carriage."

The Chevalier De Ramfay, author
of Cyrus's travels, in his plan of education for a young Prince, has (page 14.)
the following paffage to this purpofe.

" To the ftudy of poetry, fhould be
" joined that of the three arts of imi-
" tation. The antients reprefented the
" paffions,

" paffions, by gefts, colors, and founds.
" Xenophon tells us of fome wonderful
" effects of the Grecian dances, and
" how they moved and expreffed the
" paffions. We have now loft the
" perfection of that art ; all that re-
" mains, is only what is neceffary to
" give a handfome action and airs to a
" young gentleman. This ought not
" to be neglected, becaufe upon the
" external figure and appearance, de-
" pends often the regard we have to the
" internal qualities of the mind. A
" graceful behaviour, in the houfe of
" Lords or Commons, commands the
" attention of a whole affembly."

And moft certainly in this laft alle-
gation of advantage to be obtained by
a. competent fkill, or at leaft tincture
of the art, the Chevalier Ramfay, has
not exagerated its utility. Quintilian
has

has recommended it, efpecially in early years, when the limbs are the moft pliable, for procuring that fo neceffary accomplifhment, in the formation of orators gefture : obferving withall, that where that is not becoming, nothing elfe hardly pleafes.

But even independent of that confideration, nothing is more generally confeffed, than that this branch of breeding qualifies perfons for prefenting themfelves with a good grace. To whom can it be unknown that a favorable prepoffeffion at the firft fight is often of the higheft advantage; and that the power of firft impreffions is not eafily furmountable?

In affemblies or places of public refort, when we fee a perfon of a genteel carriage or prefence, he attracts our
regard

regard and liking, whether he be a
foreigner or one of this country. At
court, even a graceful addrefs, and
an air of eafe, will more diftinguifh a
man from the croud, than the richeft
cloaths that money may purchafe ; but
can never give that air to be acquired
only by education.

There are indeed who, from indolence
or felf-fufficiency, affect a fort of care-
leffnefs in their gait, as difdaining to
be obliged to any part of their education, for their external appearance,
which they abandon to itfelf under
the notion of its being natural, free,
and eafy.

But while they avoid, as they imagine,
the affectation of over-nicety, they
run into that of a vicious extreme of
negligence, which proves nothing but

S   either

either a deficiency of breeding, or if not that, a high opinion of themfelves, with what is not at all unconfequential to that, a contempt of others.

Such are certainly much miftaken, if they imagine that an art, which is principally defigned to correct defects, fhould leave fo capital an one fubfifting as that of want of eafe, and freedom, in the gefture and gait. On the contrary, it is as great an enemy to ftiffnefs, as it is to loofenefs of carriage, and air. It equally reprobates an ungainly rufticity, and a mincing, tripping, over-foft manner. Its chief aim is to bring forth the natural graces, and not to fmother them with appearances of ftudy and art.

But of all the people in the world, the Britifh would certainly be the moft

in

in the wrong for not laying a great enough ftrefs on this part of education; fince none have more confpicuoufly the merit of figure and perfon; and it would in them be a fort of ingratitude to Nature, who has done fo much for them, not to do a little more for themfelves, in acquiring an accomplifhment, the utility of which has been acknowledged in all ages, and in all countries, and efpecially by the greateft and moft fenfible men in their own.

As to the ladies, there is one light in which perhaps they would not do amifs to view the practice of this art, befides that of mere diverfion or improvement of their deportment: it is that of its being highly ferviceable to their health, and to what it can never be expected they fhould be indifferent about, their beauty, it being the beft

and

and fureſt way of preſerving, or even giving it to their whole perſon.

It is in hiſtory a ſettled point, that beauty was no where more floriſhing, nor leſs rare, than among ſuch people as encouraged and cultivated exerciſe, eſpecially in the fair ſex. The various provinces and governments in Greece, all agreed, ſome in a leſs, ſome in a greater degree, in making exerciſe a point of female education. The Spartans carried this to perhaps an exceſs, ſince the training of the children of that ſex, hardly yielded to that of the male in laborioufneſs and fatigue. Be this confeſſed to be an extreme; but then it was in ſome meaſure compenſated by its being univerſally allowed, that the Spartan women owed to it that beauty in which they excelled the reſt of the Grecian women, who were

themſelves

themſelves held, in that point, preſer-
able to the reſt of the world. Hellen
was a Spartan. Yet the legiſlator of
that people, did not ſo much as conſider
this advantage among the ends pro-
poſed in preſcribing ſo hardy an education to the weaker ſex. His views
were for giving them that health and
vigor of body, which might enable
them to produce a race of men the
fitteſt to ſerve their country in war.

But as the beſt habit of body is ever
inſeparable from the greateſt perfection
of beauty, of which its poſſeſſor is
ſuſceptible, it very naturally followed,
that the good plight to which exerciſe
brought and preſerved the females,
gave alſo to their ſhape, that delicacy
and ſuppleneſs, and to their every motion, that graceful agility which carac-
terized the Grecian beauties, and dif-
tinguiſhed

tinguifhed them for that nymph-ftile of figure, which we to this day admire in the defcription of their hiftorians, of their poets, or in the reprefentations that yet remain to us in their ftatues, or other monuments of antiquity.

But omitting to infift on the Spartan aufterity, and efpecially on their gimnaftic training for both fexes, and to take the milder methods of exercife in ufe among the Grecians, we find that the chace, that foot-races, and efpecially dancing, principally compofed the amufement of the young ladies of that country; where, in the great days of Greece, no maxim ever more practically prevailed, than that floth or inactivity was equally the parent of difeafes of the body, as of vices of the mind. Agreeable to which idea, one of the greateft phyficians now in Europe, the celebrated Tronchin,

chin, while at Paris, vehemently declaimed againſt this falſe delicacy and
averſion againſt exerciſe; from which
the ladies, eſpecially of the higher
rank of life, derived their bad habits
of body, their pale color, with all the
principles of weakneſs, and of a puny
diſeaſed conſtitution, which they ne-
ceſſarily intail on their innocent children. Thence it was that he condemned the uſing oneſelf too much
to coaches or chairs, which, he obſerved, lowers the ſpirits, thickens the
humors, numbs the nerves, and cramps
the liberty of circulation.

Conſidering the efficacy of exerciſe, and that faſhion has aboliſhed or
at leaſt confined among a very few,
the more robuſt methods of amuſement, it can hardly not be eligible
to cultivate and encourage an art, ſo

innocent

innocent and fo agreeable as that of dancing, and which at once unites in itfelf the three great ends, of bodily improvement, of diverfion, and of healthy exercife. As to this laft efpecially, it has this advantage, its being fufceptible at pleafure, of every modification, of being carried from the gentleft degree of motion, up to that of the moft violent activity. And where riding is prefcribed purely for the fake of the power of the concuffion refulting from it, to prevent or to diffipate obftructions, the fprings and agitations of the bodily frame, in the more active kind of dances, can hardly not anfwer the fame purpofe, efpecially as the motion is more equitably diffufed, and fuffers no checks or partiality from keeping the feat, as either in riding, or any other method of conveyance. At leaft, fuch an entertainment,

tainment, one would imagine, preferable, for many reasons, to an excess of such sedentary amusements as those of cards, and the like.

Certainly those of the fair sex who use exercise, will, in their exemption from a depraved or deficient appetite, in the freshness or in the glow of their color, in the firmness of their make, in the advantages to their shape, in the goodness in general of their constitution, find themselves not ill repaid for conquering any ill-habit of false delicacy and sloth, to which so many, otherwise fine young ladies, owe the disorders of their stomach, their pale sickly hue, and that languid state of health which must poison all their pleasures, and even endanger

T   their

their lives. Thefe are not ftrained nor far-fetched confequences.

But even as to thofe of either fex, the practice of dancing is attended with obvioufly good effects. Such as are bleffed by nature with a graceful fhape and are clean-limbed, receive ftill greater eafe and grace from it; while at the fame time, it prevents the gathering of thofe grofs and foggy humors which in time form a difagreeable and inconvenient corpulence. On the other hand, thofe whofe make and conftitution occafion a kind of heavy proportion, whofe mufcular texture is not diftinct, whofe necks are fhort, fhoulders round, cheft narrow, and who, in fhort are, what may be called, rather clumfy figures; thefe will greatly find their account in a competent exercife of the art of dancing, not only as it will give

them

them a freedom and eafe one would not, at the firft fight, imagine. compatible with their figure, but. may contribute much to the cure, or at leaft to the extenuation of fuch bodily defects, by giving a more free circulation to the blood, a habit of fprightlinefs and agility to the limbs, and preventing the accumulation of grofs humors, and efpecially of fat, which is itfelf not among the leaft difeafes, where it prevails to an excefs. Not that I here mean any thing fo foolifhly partial, as that nothing but dancing could operate all this ; but only place it among not the leaft efficacious means.

Nothing is more certain than that exercifes in general, diverfions, fuch as that of hunting, and the games of dexterity, keep up the natural ftandard of ftrength and beauty, which luxury and floth are fure to debafe.

Dancing

Dancing furniſhes then to the fair-
ſex, whoſe ſphere of exerciſe is naturally more confined than that of the men,
at once a ſalutary amuſement, and an
opportunity of diſplaying their native
graces. But as to men, fencing, riding
and many other improvements have
alſo doubtleſs their reſpective merit, and
anſwer very valuable purpoſes.

But where only the gentleſt exerciſe
is requiſite, the minuet offers its ſer-
vices, with the greateſt effect ; and
when elegantly executed, forms one of
the moſt agreeable ſights either in private or public aſſemblies, or, occaſio-
nally, even on the theatre itſelf.

Yet I ſpeak not of this dance here
with any purpoſe of ſpecifying rules for
for its attainment. Such an attempt
would

would be vain and impracticable. Who
does not know that almost every indivi-
dual learner requires different inſtructi-
ons ? The laying a ſtreſs on ſome particular motion or air which may be
proper to be recommended to one,
muſt be ſtrictly fobidden to another.
In ſome, their natural graces need only
to be called forth ; in others the de-
ſtroying them by affectation is to be
carefully checked. Where defects are
uncurable, the teacher muſt ſhow how
they may be palliated and ſometimes
even converted into graces. It will ea-
ſily then be granted that there is no
ſuch thing as learning a minuet, or indeed any dance merely by book. The
dead-letter of it can only be conveyed
by the noting or deſcription of the figure and of the mechanical part of it ;
but the ſpirit of it in the graces of the
air and geſture, and the carriage of the
dancer

dancer can only be practically taught
by a good master.

I have mentioned the distinction of
a good master, most assuredly not in the
way of a vain silly hint of self-recom-
dation ; but purely for the fake of giving a caution, too often neglected, a-
gainst parents, or those charged with
the education of youth, placing children, at the age when their muscles
are most flexible, their limbs the most
supple, and their minds the most duc-
tile, and who are consequently suscep-
tible of the best impressions, under
such pretended masters of this art, who
can only give them the worst, and
who, instead of teaching, stand themselves in need of being taught. The
consequence then of such a bad choice,
is, that young people of the finest dif-
position in the world, contract, under
                                    such

fuch teachers, bad, awkward habits, that are not afterwards eafily curable.

Thofe mafters who poffefs the real grounds of their art, find in their uniting their practice with their know-ledge, refources even againft the ufual depredations of age; which, though it may deprive them of fome-what of their youthful vigor, has fcarce a fenfible influence on their manner of performance. There will ftill long remain to them the traces of their former excellence.

I have myfelf feen the celebrated Dupré, at near the age of fixty, dance at Paris, with all the agility and fprightlinefs of youth, and with fuch powers of pleafing, as if the graces *in him* had braved fuperannuation.

Such

Such is the advantage of not having been content with a fuperficial tincture of this art; or with a mere rote of imitation, without an aim at excellence or originality.

But though there is no neceffity for moft learners to enter fo deep into the grounds and principles of the art, as thofe who are to make it their profeffion, it is at leaft but doing juftice to one's fcholars to give them thofe effential inftructions as to the graces of air, pofition, and gefture; without which they can never be but indifferent performers.

For example, inftead of being fo often told to turn their toes out, they fhould be admonifhed to turn their knees out, which will confequently give the true direction to the feet.

A

A due attention fhould alfo be given to the motion of the inftep, to the air of finking and rifing; to the pofition of the hips, fhoulders, and body; to the graceful management of the arms, and particularly to the giving the hand with a genteel manner, to the inflections of the neck and head, and efpecially to the fo captivating modefty of the eye; in fhort, to the diffufing over the whole execution, an air of noble eafe, and of natural gracefulnefs.

It might be too trite to mention here what is fo indifpenfable and fo much in courfe, the ftrict regard to be paid to the keeping time with the mufic.

Nothing has a better effect, nor more prepoffeffing in favor of the

U   per-

performance to follow, than the bow or curtfy at the opening the dance, made with an air of dignity and freedom. On the contrary, nothing is more difguftful than that initial ftep of the minuet, when auckwardly executed. It gives fuch an ill impreffion as is not eafily removed by even a good performance in the remaining part of the dance.

There is another point of great importance to all, but to the ladies efpecially, which is ever ftrictly recommended in the teaching of the minuet; but which in fact, like moft of the other graces of that dance, extends to other occafions of appearance in life. This point is the eafy and noble port of the head. Many very pretty ladies lofe much of the effect of their beauty, and of the fignal power

power of the firft impreffions, as they enter a room, or a public affembly, by a vulgar or improper carriage of the head, either poking the neck, or ftooping the head, or in the other extreme, of holding it up too ftiff, on the Mama's perpetually teizing remonftrance, of "hold up your head, Mifs," without confidering that merely bridling, without the eafy grace of a free play, is a worfe fault than that of which fhe will have been corrected.

Certainly nothing can give a more noble air to the whole perfon than the head finely fet, and turning gracefully, with every natural occafion for turning it, and efpecially without affectation, or ftifly pointing the chin, as if to fhow which way the wind fits.

U 2

But it muſt be impoſſible for thoſe who ſtoop their heads down, to give their figure any air of dignity, or grace of politeneſs. They muſt always retain ſomething of ignoble in their manner. Nothing then is more recommendable than for thoſe who are naturally inclined to this defect, to endeavor the avoiding it by a particular attention to this capital inſtruction in learning the minuet. It is alſo not enough to take the minuet-ſteps true to time, to turn out their knees, and to ſlide their ſtep neatly, if that flexibility, or riſe and fall from the graceful bending of the inſtep, is not attended to, which gives ſo elegant an air to the execution either of the minuet, or of the ſerious theatrical dances. Nothing can more than that, ſet off or ſhow the beauty of the ſteps.

It

It should also be recommended to the dancers of the minuet, ever to have an expreffion of that fort of gaity and chearfulnefs in the countenance, which will give it an amiable and even a noble franknefs. Nothing can be more out of character, or even dif-pleafing, than a froward or too penfive a look. There may be a fprightly va-cancy, an opennefs in the face, with-out the leaft tincture of any indecent air of levity : as there may be a capti-vating modefty, without any of that bafhfulnefs which arifes either from low breeding, wrong breeding, or no breed-ing at all.

But to execute a minuet in a very fuperior manner, it is recommendable to enter into fome acquaintance, at leaft, with the principles of the ferious or grave dances, with a naturally genteel perfon,

perfon, a fuperficial knowledge of the
fteps, and a fmattering of the rules,
any one almoft may foon be made to
acquit himfelf tolerably of a minuet;
but to make a diftinguifhed figure, fome
notion of the depths and refinements
of the art, illuftrated by proper practice, are required.

It is efpecially incumbent on an
artift, not to reft fatisfied with having
pleafed : he fhould, from his knowledge of the grounds of his art, be able
to tell himfelf why he has pleafed;
and thus by building upon folid principles, preferably to mere lucky hits,
or to tranfient and accidental advantages of form or manner, infure the
permanency of his power to pleafe.

There is a vice in dancing, againft
which pupils cannot be too carefully
guarded;

guarded; it is that of affectation. It is essentially different from that desire of pleasing, which is so natural and so consistent even with the greatest modesty, in that it always builds on some falsity, mistaken for a means of pleasing, though nothing can more surely defeat that intention; there is not an axiom more true than that the graces are incompatible with affectation. They vanish at the first appearance of it: and the curse of affectation is, that it never but lets itself be seen, and wherever it is seen, it is sure to offend, and to frustrate its own design.

The simplicity of nature is the great fountain of all the graces; from which they flow spontaneous, when unchecked by affectation, which at once poisons and dries them up.

Nature

Nature does not refuse cultivation, but she will not·bear being forced. The great art of the dancing-master is not to give graces, for that is impoffible, but to call forth into a nobly modeft difplay thofe latent ones in his fcholars, which may have been buried for want of op-portunities or of education to break forth in their native luftre, or which have been fpoiled or perverted, by wrong inftruction, or by bad models of imitations. In this laft cafe, the mafter's bufinefs is rather to extirpate than to plant; to clear the ground of poifonous exotics, and to make way for the pleafing productions of na-ture.

This admirable prerogative of pleaf-ing, infeparable from the natural graces, unpoifoned by affectation, is in nothing more ftrongly exemplified, than

than in the rural dances, where fimplicity of manners, a fprightly eafe, and
an exemption from all defign but that
of innocent mirth, give to the young
and handfome villagers, or country-
maids, thofe inimitable graces for ever
unknown to artifice and affectation.
Not but, even in thofe rural affemblies,
there may be found fome characters
tainted with affectation ; but then in
the country they are exceptions, whereas in town they conftitute the generality, who are fo apt to miftake airs
for graces, though nothing can be more
effentially different.

But how fhall thofe mafters guard
a fcholar fufficiently againft affectation,
who are themfelves notorioufly infected
with it ?   Nay, this is fo common to
them, that it is even the foundation of
a proverbial remark, that no gentle-

X   man

man can be faid to dance well, who
dances like a dancing-mafter.   Thofe
falfe refinements, that finical, affected
air fo juftly reproached to the generality of teachers, a mafter fhould correct
in himfelf before he can well give
leffons for avoiding them to his pupils.
And, in truth, they are but wretched
fubftitutes to the true grounds and
principles of the art, in which nothing
is more ftongly inculcated than the total
neglect of them, and the reliance on the
engaging and noble fimplicity of nature.

It is then no paradox to fay that the
more deep you are in the art, the lefs
will it ftifle nature.   On the contrary,
it will, in the noble affurance which a
competent fkill is fure to bring with it,
give to the natural graces a greater freedom and eafe of difplay.   Imperfection
of

of theory and practice cramps the faculties ; and gives either an unpleasing
faulteringness to the air, steps, and gestures, or wrong execution. And as
the minuet derives its merit from an
observation of the most agreeable steps,
well chosen in nature and well combin-
ed by art, there is no inconsistence in
avering that art may, in this, as in
many other objects of imitative skill,
essentially assist nature, and place
her in the most advantageous point of
light.

The truth of this will be easily
granted, by numbers who have felt the
pleasure of seeing a minuet gracefully
executed by a couple who understood
this dance perfectly. Nay, excellence
in the performance of it, has given to
an indifferent figure, at least a temporary advantage over a much superior one

X 2   in

in point of perſon only ; and ſometimes an advantage of which the impreſſion has been more permanent.

But beſides the effect of the moment in pleaſing the ſpectators ; the being well verſed in this dance eſpecially contributes greatly to form the gait, and addreſs, as well as the manner in which we ſhould preſent ourſelves. It has a ſenſible influence in the poliſhing and faſhioning the air and deportment in all occaſions of appearance in life. It helps to wear off any thing of clowniſhneſs in the carriage of the perſon, and breathes itſelf into otherwiſe the moſt indifferent actions, in a genteel and agreeable manner of performing them.

This ſecret and relative influence of the minuet, *Marcel,* my ever re-
ſpected

ſpeded maſter, whom his own merit
in his profeſſion, and the humorous
mention of him by *Helvetius*, in his
famous book DE L'ESPRIT, have
made ſo well known, conſtantly kept
in view, in his method of teaching it.
His ſcholars were generally known and
diſtinguiſhed from thoſe of other maſters, not only by their excellence in
adual dancing, but by a certain ſupe-
rior air of eaſy-genteelneſs at other
times. He himſelf danced the minuet
to its utmoſt perfedion. Not that
he confined his pradice to that dance
alone; on the contrary, he confeſſed
himſelf obliged for his greateſt ſkill in
that, to his having a general knowledge of all the other dances, which he
had pradiſed, but eſpecially thoſe of
the ſerious ſtile.

But

But certainly it is not only to the profeffed dancer, that dancing in the ferious ftile, or the minuet, with grace and eafe, is effential. The poffeffing this branch of dancing is of great fervice on the theatre, even to an actor. The effect of it fteals into his manner, and gait, and gives him an air of prefenting himfelf, that is fure to prepoffefs in his favor. Perfons of of every fize or fhape are fufceptible of grace and improvement from it. The fhoulders fo drawn back as not to protuberate before, but as it were, to retreat from fight, or as the French exprefs it *bien effacées*, the knees well turning outwards, with a free play; the air of the fhape noble and difengaged; the turns and movements eafy; in fhort, all the graces that characterife a good execution of the minuet, will, infenfibly on all other occafions, diftribute through

every

every limb and part of the body, a certain liberty and agreeablenefs of motion eafier to be conceived than de-
fined. To the actor, in all characters,
it gives, as I have juft before obferved,
a graceful mien and prefence ; but, in
ferious characters, it efpecially fuggefts
that ftriking portlinefs, that majeftic
tread of the ftage, for which fome
actors from the very firft of their ap-
appearance fo happily difpofe the public to a favorable reception of their
merit in the reft of their part. An influence of the firft impreffion, which a
good actor will hardly defpife, efpecially with due precaution againft his
contracting any thing forced or affected in his air or fteps, from his attention to his improvement by dancing,
as the very beft things may be even
pernicious by a mifufe. Whatever is
not natural, free, and eafy, will undoubtedly

doubtedly, on the ſtage, as every where elſe, have a bad effect. A very little matter of exceſs will, from his aim at a grace, produce a ridiculous caricature. Too ſtiff a regulation of his motions or geſtures, by meaſure and cadence, would even be worſe than abandoning every thing to chance; which might, like the Eolian harp, ſometimes ſuffer lucky hits to eſcape him; whereas affectation is as ſure forever to diſpleaſe, as it is not to eſcape the being ſeen where it exiſts.

Among the many reaſons for this dance of the minuet having become general, is the poſſibility of dancing it to ſo many different airs, though the ſteps are invariable. If one tune does not pleaſe a performer, he may call for another; the minuet ſtill remaining unalterable.

There

There is no occafion however for a learner to be con fined to this dance. He fhould rather be encouraged, or have a curiofity be excited in him, to learn efpecially thofe dances, which are of the more tender or ferious character, contributing, as they greatly do, to perfect one in the minuet; independently of the pleafure they befides give both in the performance and to the fight. The dances the moft in requeft are, the *Saraband,* the *Bretagne* the *Furlana,* the *Paſſepied,* the *Folie d'Eſpagne,* the *Rigaudon,* the *Minuet du Dauphin* the *Louvre, La Mariée,* which is always danced at the Opera of Roland at Paris. Some of thefe are performed folo, others are duet-dances. The *Louvre* is held by many the moft pleafing of them all, efpecially when well executed by both performers, in a juft concert of motions; no dance affor-

Y   ding

ding the arms more occafion for. a graceful difplay of them, or a more delicate regularity of the fteps; being compofed of the moft felect ones from theatrical dances, and formed upon the trueft principles of the art. This dance is executed in moft countries of Europe without any variation. It is generally, followed or terminated by a minuet; and thefe two dances, the Louvre and the minuet, are at prefent the moft univerfally in fafhion, and will, in all probability, continue fo, from their being both pleafing beyond all others, to the performers, as well as to the fpectators, and from their not being difficult to learn, if the fcholar has but common docility.

Youth being for learning this art undoubtedly the beft feafon, for reafons as I have before obferved, too

obvious

obvious to need infifting on, the mafter cannot pay too much atten- tion to the availing himfelf of the pliancy of that age, to give his fcho- lars the neceffary inftructions for pre- paring and well-difpofing their limbs. This holds good, particularly with re- gard to that propenfity innate to moft perfons of turning in their toes. I have already mentioned the expedi- ency of curing this defect, by the di- recting them to acquire a habit of turning the knees outward, to which I have to add, that on the proper turn of the knee, chiefly depend the graces of the under part of the fi- gure, that is to fay, from the foot to the hip.

Frequent practice alfo of dancing, or of any falutary exercife, is alfo highly recommendable for obtaining a firm-

nefs

nefs of body ; for a tottering dancer can never plant his fteps fo as to afford a pleafing execution. It may found a little odd, but, the truth is, that in dancing, fprightlinefs and a-gility are principally produced by bo-dily ftrength ; while on the contrary, weaknefs, or infirmity, muft give every ftep and fpring, not only a tottering, but a heavy air. The legs that bear with the moft eafe the weight of the body, will naturally make it feem the lighteft.

A

A

SUMMARY ACCOUNT

Of various kinds of

D A N C E S

In different Parts of the WORLD.

Cantatur et faltatur apud omnes gentes, aliquo faltem modo,   QUINT.

I N

E U R O P E.

AS almoſt every country has dances particular to it, or, at leaſt,
ſo naturalized by adoption from others,

that

that in length of time they pafs for originals; a flight fketch of the moft remarkable of them may ferve to throw a light upon this fubject, entertaining to fome, and both entertaining and ufeful to others.

In BRITAIN, you have the horn-pipe, a dance which is held an original of this country. Some of the fteps of it are ufed in the country-dances here, which are themfelves a kind of dance executed with more variety and agreeablenefs than in any part of Europe, where they are alfo imitatively performed, as in Italy, Germany and in feveral other countries. Nor is it without reafon they obtain, here the preference over the like in other places. They are no where fo well executed. The mufic is extremely well adapted, and the fteps in general
neral

neral are very pleafing. Some foreign comic dancers, on their coming here, apply themfelves with great attention to the true ftudy of the hornpipe, and by conftant practice acquire the ability of performing it with fuccefs in foreign countries, where it always meets with the higheft applaufe, when mafterly executed. There was an inftance of this, fometime ago at Venice, at an opera there, when the theatre was as well provided with good fingers and dancers, as any other. But they had not the good fortune to pleafe the public. A dancer luckily for the manager, prefented himfelf, who danced the hornpipe in its due perfection. This novelty took fo, and made fuch full houfes, that the manager, who had begun with great lofs, foon faw himfelf repaired, and was

a

a gainer when he little expected
it.

It is to the HIGHLANDERS in
North-Britain, that I am told we are
indebted for a dance in the comic
vein, called the *Scotch Reel*, executed
generally, and I believe always in
trio, or by three. When well danced,
it has a very pleafing effect: and
indeed nothing can be imagined more
agreeable, or more lively and brilliant,
than the fteps in many of the Scotch
dances. There is a great variety of
very natural and very pleafing ones.
And a compofer of comic dances,
might, with great advantage to himfelf,
upon a judicious affemblage of fuch
fteps as he might pick out of their
dances, form a dance that, with well
adapted dreffes, correfpondent mufic,
and figures capable of a juft performance,

ance, could hardly fail of a great fuccefs upon the theatre.

I do not know whether I fhall not
ftand in need of an apology for mentioning here a dance once popular in
England, but to which the idea of
low is now currently annexed. It was
originally adapted from the Moors,
and is ftill known by the name of
Morris-dancing, or Morefc-dance. It
is danced with fwords, by perfons odly difguifed, with a great deal of antic rural merriment : it is true that
this diverfion is now almoft exploded,
being entirely confined to the lower
claffes of life, and only kept up in fome
counties. What the reafon may be
of its going out of ufe, I cannot fay ;
but am very fure, there was not only
a great deal of natural mirth in it,
but that it is fufceptible enough of

Z   im-

improvement, to rescue it from the contempt it may have incurred, through its being chiefly in use among the vulgar; though most probably it may have descended among them from the higher ranks. For certainly of them it was not quite unworthy, for the Pirrhic or military air it carries with it, and which probably was the cause of its introduction among so martial a people. Rude, as it was, it might require refinement, but it did not, perhaps, deserve to become quite obsolete.

In SPAIN, they have a dance, called, *Les Folies d'Espagne*, which is performed either by one or by two, with castanets. There is a dress peculiarly adapted to it, which has a very pleasing effect, as well as the dance itself.

In

In FRANCE, their *Contre-dances,* are drawn from the true principles of the art, and the figures and fteps are generally very agreeable. No nation cultivates this art with more tafte and delicacy. Their *Provençale* dance, is moft delightfully fprightly, and well imagined. The fteps feem to correfpond with the natural vivacity and gaiety of the Provençals. This dance is commonly performed to the pipe and tabor.

The FLEMISH dances run in the moft droll vein of true rural humor. The performers feem to be made for the dances, and the dances for the performers; fo well afforted are the figures to the reprefentation. Several eminent painters in the grotefque ftile, Teniers efpecially, have formed many divert-

Z 2　　　　　　　　　ing

ing pictures taken from life, upon this
fubject.

At NAPLES, they have various grotefque dances, which are originals in
their kind, being extremely difficult to
execute, not only for the variety of the
fteps, but for the intricacy and uncom-
monnefs, or rather fingularity of them.

But while I am mentioning Naples, I
ought not to omit that effect of dancing,
which is attributed to it, upon thofe
who are bitten with the *Tarantula*.
The original of this opinion, was probably owing to fome fenfible phyfician,
prefcribing fuch a violent motion, more
likely to be kept up in the patient, by
the power of mufic, than by any thing
elfe, as might enable him to expel the
poifon, by being thereby thrown into
a copious fweat, and by other benefits
from

from fuch a vehement agitation. This,
it is fuppofed, was afterwards abufed
and turned into a mere trick, to affemble
a croud and get money, either by fham
bites, or by making a kind of fhow of
this method of practice in real ones.
However, that may be, the various
grimaces or contortions, leaps and irre-
gular fteps, commonly ufed on this occafion, to be executed to that fort of
mufic, or airs adapted to it, might afford a good fubject for a grotefque dance,
to be formed upon the plan of a burlefque or mock-imitation : and I am
not quite fure that the idea of fuch a
dance, has not been already carried into
execution.

The caftanets the NEAPOLITANS
moft frequently ufe, are of the largeft
fize. It is alfo from Naples that we have
taken the Punchinello dance.

At

At FLORENCE, they have a dance, called, *il Treschone.* The country-women, in the villages, are very fond of it. They are generally speaking, very robust, and capable of holding out the fatigue of this dance, for a long time. To make themselves more light for it, they often pull off their shoes. The dance is opened by a couple, one of each sex. The woman holds in her hand a handkerchief, which she flings to him whom she chuses for her next partner, who, in his turn has an equal right to dispose of it in the same manner, to any woman of the company he chuses. Thus is the dance carried on without any interruption till the affembly breaks up.

The favorite dance of the VENETI-ANS, is what they call the *Furlana,* which is performed by two persons dancing a-round a-round with the greateſt rapidity. Thoſe who have a good ear, keep time with the croſſing their feet behind; and ſome add a motion of their hands, as if they were rowing or tugging at an oar. This dance is practiced in ſeveral other parts of Italy.

The Peaſants of TIROL, have one of the moſt pleaſant and groteſque dances that can be imagined. They perform it in a ſort of holy-day dreſs, made of ſkins, and adorned with ribbons. They wear wooden ſhoes, not uncuriouſly painted; and the women eſpecially ex-preſs a kind of rural ſimplicity and frolic mirth, which has a very agreeable effect.

The GRISONS are in poſſeſſion of an old dance, which is not without its merit, and which they would not ex-change

change for the politeſt in Europe; they
being as invariably attached to it, as to
their dreſs.

The HUNGARIANS are very noiſy in
their dances, with their iron heels, but
when they are of an equal ſize, and
dreſſed in their uniforms, the agility
of their ſteps, and the regularity of
dreſs in the performers, render them
not a diſagreeable ſight.

The GERMANS have a dance called
the *Allemande,* in which the men and
women form a ring. Each man holding his partner round the waiſt, makes
her whirl round with almoſt incon-
ceivable rapidity: they dance in a grand
circle, ſeeming to purſue one another:
in the courſe of which they execute
ſeveral leaps, and ſome particularly
pleaſing ſteps, when they turn, but ſo
very

very difficult as to appear fuch even to profeffed dancers themfelves. When this dance is performed by a numerous company, it furnifhes one of the moft pleafing fights that can be imagined.

The Polish nobility have a dance, to which the magnificence of their drefs, and the elegance of the fteps, the gracefulnefs of the attitudes, the fitnefs of the mufic, all contribute to produce a great effect. Were it performed here on the theatre, it would hardly fail of a general applaufe.

The Cossacs, have, amidft all their uncouth barbarifm, a fort of dancing, which they execute to the found of an inftrument, fomewhat refembling a Mandoline, but confiderably larger, and which is highly diverting, from the extreme vivacity of the fteps, and the

A a   oddity

oddity of the contortions and grimaces, with which they exhibit it. For a grotefque dance there can hardly be imagined any thing more entertaining.

The RUSSIANS, afford nothing remarkable in their dances, which they now chiefly take from other countries. The dance of dwarfs with which the Czar Peter the Great, folemnized the nuptials of his niece to the Duke of Courland, was, probably rather a particular whim of his own, than a national ufage.

I N

IN Turky, dances have been, as of old in Greece, and elsewhere instituted in form of a religious ceremony. The *Dervishes* who are a kind of devotionists execute a dance, called the *Semaat* in a circle, to a strange wild-simphony, when holding one another by the hand, they turn round with such rapidity, that, with pure giddiness, they often fall down in heaps upon one another.

A a 2   They

They have alſo in Turky, as well as India and Perſia, profeſſed dancers, eſpecially of the female ſex, under the name of dancing-girls, who are bred up, from their childhood, to the profeſſion ; and are always ſent for to any great entertainment, public or private, as at feaſts, weddings, ceremonies of circumciſion, and, in ſhort, on all occaſions of feſtivity and joy. They execute their dances to a ſimphony of various inſtruments, extremely reſembling the antient ones, the *tympanum*, the *crotala*, the *cimbals*, and the like, as well as to ſongs, being a kind of ſmall dramatic compoſitions. or what may properly be called *ballads*, which is, a true word for a ſong at once ſung and danced : *ballare* ſignifying to dance; and *ballata*, a ſong, compoſed to be danced. It is probable that from theſe eaſtern kind of dances, which are undoubtedly

doubtedly very antient, came the name,
among the Romans, of *balatrones*.
Nothing can be imagined more graceful,
nor more expreſſive, than the geſtures
and attitudes of thoſe dancing-girls,
which may properly be called the
eloquence of the body, in which indeed moſt of the Aſiatics and inhabitants of the ſouthren climates conſtitu-
tionally excel, from a ſenſibility more
exquiſite than, is the attribute of the
more northern people ; but a ſenſibility ballanced by too many diſadvanta-
ges to be envied them. The Sia-
meſe, we are told, have three dances,
called the *Cone*, the *Lacone*, and the
Raban. The *Cone* is a figure-dance, in
which they uſe particularly a ſtring-
inſtrument in the nature of a violin,
with ſome others of the Aſiatic make.
Thoſe who dance are armed and maſk-
ed, and ſeem to be a fighting rather
than

than dancing. It is a kind of Indian Pirrhic. Their maſks repreſent the moſt frightful hideous countenances of wild-beaſts, or demons, that fancy can invent. In the *Lacone* the performers ſing commutually ſtanzes of verſes containing the hiſtory of their country. The Raban is a mixed dance, of men and women, not martial, nor hiſtorical, but purely gallant ; in which the dancers have all long falſe nails of copper. They ſing in this dance, which is only a ſlow march without any high motions, but with a great many contortions of body and arms. Thoſe who dance in the Raban and Cone have high gilt caps like ſugar-loaves. The dance of the *Lacone* is appropriated to the dedication of their temples, when a new ſtatue of their *Sommona-codom* is ſet up.

In

In many parts of the Eaft, at their weddings, in conducting the bride from her houfe to the bridegroom's, as in Perfia efpecially, they make ufe of proceffional mufic and dancing. But, in the religious ceremonies of the Gentoos, when, at ftated times, they draw the triumphal car, in which the image of the deity of the feftival is carried, the proceffion is intermixed with troops of dancers of both fexes, who, proceed, in chorus, leaping, dancing, and falling into ftrange antics, as the proceffion moves along, of which they compofe a part ; thefe adapt their geftures and fteps to the founds of various inftruments of mufic.

Confidering withal that the Romans, in their moft folemn proceffions, as in that called the *Pompa*, whichI have before mentioned, in which not only the

Pirrhic

Pirrhic dance was proceffionally executed, but other dances, in mafquerade,
by men who, in their habits, by leaping and by feats of agility, reprefented
fatirs, the *Sileni,* and *Fauni,* and were
attended by minftrels playing on the flute
and guitar; befides which, there were
Salian priefts, and *Salian* virgins, who followed, in their order, and executed their
refpective religious dances; it may bear
a queftion whether not an unpleafing ufe
might not be made, on the theatres, of
proceffional dances properly introduced,
and connected, efpecially in the burlefque way. In every country, and particularly in this, proceffions are efteemed an agreeable amufement to the eye;
and certainly they muft receive more
life and animation from a proper inter-
mixture of dances, than what a mere
folemn march can reprefent, where there
is nothing to amufe but a long train of
                                    perfonages

perfonages in various habits, walking in parade. I only mention this however as a hint not impoffible to be improved, and reduced into practice.

But even, where it might be improper or ridiculous to think of mixing dances with a proceffion, though it were but in burlefque, which muft, if at all, be the preferable way of mixing them, the pleafure of thofe who delight in feeing proceffions and pageantry exhibited on the theatre, might be gratified, without any violence to propriety, by making them introductory to the dances of the grandeft kind. For example ; where a dance in Chinefe characters is intended, a proceffion might be previoufly brought in, of perfonages, of whom the habits, charactures, and manners might be faithfully copied from nature, and from the truth of

B b   things

things, and convey to the spectator
a juster notion of the people from
which the reprefentation was taken,
of their drefs and public proceffions,
than any verbal defcription, or even
prints or pictures. After which, the
dance might naturally take place, in
celebration of the feftival, of which
the proceffion might be fuppofed the
occafion.

In order to give a more diftinct
idea of this hint, I have hereto annexed the print of a Chinefe proceffion taken from the defcription of a
traveller into that country; by which
a good compofer would well know
how to make a proper choice of
what might be exhibited, and what
was fit to be left out; efpecially according as the dance fhould be, ferious or burlefque. In the laft cafe;

even

even the horfes might be reprefented
by a theatrical imitation. And certainly, bringing the perfonages on
in fuch a regular proceffion at firft,
would give a better opportunity of
obferving their dreffes, than in the
huddled, confufed manner of grouping them, that has been fometimes
practifed : to fay nothing of the pleafure afforded to the eye by the proceffion itfelf.

The print annexed reprefents the
proceffion of a Chinefe Mandarin of
the firft order. Firft appear two men
who ftrike each upon a copper inftrument called a gongh, refembling a hollow difh without a border, which has
pretty much the effect of a kettle-drum.

Follow the enfign-bearers, on whofe
flags are written in large characters
B b 2   the

the Mandarin's titles of honour. Next fourteen ftandards, upon' which appear the proper fimbols of his office, fuch as the dragon, tiger, phœnix, flying tortoife, and other winged creatures of fancy, emblematically exhibited.

Six officers, bearing a ftaff headed by an oblong fquare board, raifed high, whereon are written in large golden characters the particular qualities of this Mandarin.

Two others bear, the one a large umbrella of yellow filk (the imperial color) of three folds, one above the other; the other officer carries the cafe in which the umbrella is kept.

Two archers on horfeback, at the head of the chief guard: then the guards

guards, armed with large hooks, adorned with filk fringe, in four rows one above another; two other files of men in armor, fome bearing maces with long handles; others, maces in the form of a hand, or of a ferpent: others, equipped with large hammers and long hatchets like a crefcent. Other guards bearing fharp axes: fome, weapons like fcythes, only ftrait. Soldiers carrying three-edged halberds.

Two porters, carrying a fplendid coffer, containing the feal of his office.

Two other men, beating each a *gongh*, which gives notice of the Mandarin's approach.

Two officers, armed with ftaves, to keep off the croud.

Two

Two mace-bearers with gilt maces in the fhape of dragons, and a number of officers of juftice, fome equiped with bamboes, a kind of flat cudgels, to give the baftinado: others with chains, whips, cutlaffes, and hangers.

Two ftandard-bearers, and the captain of the guard.

All this equipage precedes the Mandarin or Viceroy, who is carried in his chair, furrounded with pages and footmen, having near his perfon an officer who carries a large fan in the fhape of a hand-fire-fcreen.

He is followed by guards, fome armed with maces, and others with long-handled fabres; after whom come feveral enfigns and cornets, with a great

great number of domeſtics on horſe-
back, every one bearing ſome neceſſary belonging to the Mandarin:
as for example, a particular Tartarian
cap, if the weather ſhould oblige
him to change the one he has on.

From the above, it may appear,
what ſcope or range a compoſer may
have for the exhibition of proceſſions
and pageantry of other nations, as
well as of the Chineſe; in all which,
nothing is more recommendable than
adhering, in the repreſentation, as
much as the limitations of the theatre will admit, to the truth of things,
as they actually paſs in the countries where the ſcene is laid: which
is but, in ſaying other words, in this,
as in every other imitative branch,
ſtrike to nature as cloſe as poſſible.

I N

I N

A F R I C A.

THE spirit of dancing prevails, almost beyond imagination, among both men and women, in most parts of Africa. It is even more than instinct, it is a rage, in some countries of that part of the globe.

Upon the Gold-coast especially, the inhabitants are so passionately fond of it, that in the midst of their hardest labor, if they hear a person
sing,

fing, or any mufical inftrument plaid, they cannot refrain from dancing.

There are even well attefted ftories of fome Negroes flinging themfelves at the feet of an European playing on a fiddle, entreating him to defift, unlefs he had a mind to tire them to death ; it being impoffible for them to ceafe dancing, while he continued playing. Such is the irrefiftible paffion for dancing among them.

With fuch an innate fondnefs for this art, one would imagine that children taken from this country, fo ftrong-made and fo well-limbed as they generally are, and fo finely difpofed by nature, might, if duly inftructed, go great lengths towards perfection in the art. But I do not remember to have heard that the experiment

ment was ever made upon any of them, by fome mafter capable of giving them fuch an improvement, as one would fuppofe them fufceptible of.

Upon the Gold-coaft, there long exifted and probably ftill exifts a cuftom, for the greater part of the inhabitants of a town or village to affemble together, moft evenings of the year, at the market-place to dance, fing, and make merry for an hour or two, before bed-time. On this occafion, they appear in their beft attire. The women, who come before the men, have a number of little bells tinkling at their feet. The men carry little fans or rather whifks in their hand made of the tails of elephants and horfes, much like the brufhes ufed to brufh pictures; only that theirs are gilt at both

Cc 2   ends.

ends. They meet ufually about fun-
fet. Their mufic confifts of horn-blow-
ers or trumpeters, drummers, players
on the flute, and the like ; being placed
a-part by themfelves. The men and
women, who compofe the dance, di-
vide into couples, facing each other,
as in our country-dances, and forming
a general dance, fall into many wild
ridiculous poftures, advancing and re-
treating, leaping, ftamping on the
ground, bowing their heads, as they
pafs, to each other, and muttering certain words; then fnapping their fingers,
fometimes fpeaking loud, at other times
whifpering, moving now flow, now
quick, and fhaking their fans.

Artus and Villault add, that they
ftrike each another's fhoulders alternately with thofe fans ; alfo that the
women, laying ftraw-ropes in circles on
the

the ground, jump into or dance round them ; and clicking them up with their toes, caſt them in the air, catching them as they fall with their hands.

They are ſtrangely delighted with theſe gambols ; but do not care to be ſeen at them by ſtrangers, who can ſcarce refrain laughing, and conſe-quently putting them out of counte-nance.

After an hour or two ſpent in this kind of exerciſe, they retire to their reſpective homes.

Their dances vary according to times, occurrences, and places. Thoſe which are in honor of their religious feſtivals, are more grave and ſerious. There have been ſometimes public dances inſtituted by order of their Kings, as at Abrambo, a large

214 A TREATISE ON THE

a large town in Widaw, where an-
nually, for eight days together, there
reforted a multitude of both fexes from
all parts of the country. This was
called the dancing-feafon. To this
folemnity all came dreffed in the beft
manner, according to their refpective
ability. The dance was ridiculous
enough ; but it ferved to keep up their
agility of body. And amidft all the
uncouth barbarifm of their geftures and
attitudes, nature breaks out into fome
expreffions of joy, or of the paffions, that
would not be unworthy of an European's obfervation.

They have alfo their kind of Pirrhic
dances, which they execute by mock-
fkirmifhing in cadence, and ftriking
on their targets with their cutlaffes.

I have

I have already mentioned that it is from Africa, the Moresc-dances originally came. But what is somewhat surprising, the Portugueze themselves, among whom I will not however include the higher ranks of life in that nation, but, at least, the number of the people who adopted, from the Caffrees, or Negroes of their African possessions, a dance called by them *LasCheganças*, (Approaches) was so great that the late King of Portugal was obliged to prohibit it by a formal edict. The reason of which was, that some of the motions and gestures had so lascivious an air, and were so contrary to modesty, that the celebrated *Frey Gaspar*, a natural son, if I mistake not, of the late King of Portugal, represented so efficaciously to his Portugueze Majesty, the shame and scandal of this dance being any longer suffered,

fered, that it was put down by royal
authority. Nor was this done without
occasioning heavy complaints againſt
Frey Gaſpar, againſt whom there were
lampoons and ballads publickly ſung,
upon his having uſed his influence to
procure that prohibition.

I N

A M E R I C A.

IN this part of the world, ſo lately diſcovered, nothing is a ſtronger proof of the univerſality of dancing, of its being, in ſhort, rather an human inſtinct, than an art, than the fondneſs for dancing every where diffuſed over this vaſt continent.

D d In

In BRAZIL, the dancers, whether men or women, make a point of dancing bare-headed. The reaſon of this is not mentioned : it cannot however be thought a very ſerious one, ſince nothing can be more comical than their geſtures, their contortions of body, and the ſigns they make with the head to each other.

In MEXICO, they have alſo their dances and muſic, but in the moſt uncouth and barbarian ſtile. For their ſimphony they have wooden drums, ſomething in form of a kettle-drum, with a kind of pipe or flageolet, made of a hollow cane or reed, but very grating to an European ear. It is obſerved they love every thing that makes a noiſe how diſagreeable ſoever the ſound is. They will alſo hum over ſomething like a tune, when they dance

thirty

thirty or forty in a circle, stretching out their hands, and laying them on each others shoulders. They stamp and jump, and use the most antic gestures for several hours, till they are heartily weary. And one or two of the company sometimes step out of the ring, to make sport for the rest, by showing feats of activity, throwing up their lances into the air, catching them again, bending backwards, and springing forwards with great agility. Then when they are in a violent sweat, from this exercise, they will frequently jump into the water, without the least bad consequences to their health. Their women have their dancing and music too by themselves; but never mingle in those of the men.

In VIRGINIA, according to the author of the history of that country,

D d 2

they

they have two different kinds of dancing ; the firſt, either ſingle, or at the
moſt in ſmall companies ; or, ſecondly,
in great numbers together, but without
having any regard either to time or
figure.

In the firſt kind one perſon only
dances, or two, or three at moſt. While
during their performance, the reſt, who
are ſeated round them in a ring, ſing
as loud as they can ſcream, and ring
their little bells. Sometimes the dancers
themſelves ſing, dart terribly threaten-
ing looks, ſtamp their feet upon the
ground, and exhibit a thouſand antic
poſtures and grimaces.

In the other dance, conſiſting of a
more numerous company of performers,
the dance is executed round ſtakes
ſet in the form of a circle, adorned
with

with fome fculpture, or round about a
fire, which they light in a convenient
place. Every one has his little bell,
his bow and arrow in his hand.
They alfo cover themfelves with leaves,
and thus equipped, begin their dance.
Sometimes they fet three young women in the midft of the circle.

In PERU, the manner of dancing
has fomething very particular. Inftead
of laying any ftrefs on the motion
of the arms, in moft of their dances,
their arms hang down, or are wrap-
ped up in a kind of mantle, fo that
nothing is feen but the bending of
the body, and the activity of the feet;
they have however many figure-dan-
ces, in which they lay afide their cloaks
or mantles, but the graces they add,
are rather actions than geftures.

The

The PERUVIAN Creolians dance after the fame manner, without laying afide their long fwords, the point of which they contrive to keep up before them fo that it may not hinder them from rifing, or in coupeeing, which is fometimes to fuch a degree that it looks like kneeling.

They have a dance there, adopted from the natives, which they call *Zapatas*, (fhoes) becaufe in dancing they alternately ftrike with the heels and toes, taking fome fteps, and coupeeing, as they traverfe their ground.

Among the favages of North-America, we are told there are various dances practifed, fuch as that of the calumet, the leaders dance, the war-dance, the marriage-dance, the facrifice-dance, all which, refpectively differ in the movements,

ments, and fome, amidft all the wild-
nefs of their performance, are not
without their graces. But the dance
of the calumet is efteemed the fineft ;
this is ufed at the reception of ftrangers
whom they mean to honor, or of
ambaffadors to them on public occafions. This dance is commonly
executed in an oval figure.

The AMERICANS, in fome parts,
prefcribe this exercife by way of
phific, in their diftempers : a method
of treatment, not, it feems unknown
to the antients : but, in general, their
motive for dancing, is the fame as
with the reft of the world, to give de-
monftrations of joy and welcome to
their guefts, or to divert themfelves.
On fome occafions indeed, they make
them part of the ceremony at their
affemblies upon affairs, when even
their

their public debates are preceded by
dancing, as if they expected that that
exercife would roufe their mental faculties, and clear their heads. The
war-dance is alfo ufed by them, by
way of proclamation of war againft
their enemies.

The foregoing fummary fketch of
fome of the various dances, which
are practifed in different parts of
the globe, and which, to defcribe
univerfally and minutely, would fill
whole volumes, may ferve to fhow
that nature has, in all parts of the
inhabited world, given to man the
inftinct of dancing, as well as of
fpeaking, or of finging. But it certainly depends on the nations who
encourage the polite arts, once more
to carry it up to that pitch of excellence, of which the hiftory of the
Greeks

Greeks and Romans fhows it to have been fufceptible, among the antients, however the moderns may have long fallen fhort of it. There has indeed lately appeared a dawning hope of its recovery; which, that it may not be fruftrated, is the intereft of all who wifh well to an innocent and even ufeful pleafure.

E e   O F

O F

PANTOMIMES.

AS this branch of the art of dancing is often mentioned, efpecially in this country, without a juft
idea being affixed to it, or any other
idea than what is vulgarly taken from
a fpecies of compofitions which are
fometimes exhibited after the play, on
the theatre here, (not to mention Sad-
ler's wells) and go by the name of
pantomime entertainments; it may not
be unacceptable to the reader, my lay-

ing

ing down before him the true grounds
and nature of this diverfion, which
once made fo great a figure in the
theatrical fphere of action.

And as, on this point, Monfieur
Cahufac, an ingenious French writer,
has treated the hiftorical part of it with
fo much accuracy, that it was hardly
poffible to offer any thing new upon it,
beyond what he has furnifhed ; and
that not to make ufe of his refearches
would only betray me into a fruitlefs
affectation of originality, I am very
ready to confefs, that for the beft and
greateft part of what I am now going
to offer upon this fubject I am indebted
to his production.

That prodigious perfection to which
the antients carried the pantomime art,
appeared fo extraordinary to the celebrated

229 ART OF DANCING.

brated abbot Du Bos, that, not be
ing able to contradict the authorities
which eſtabliſh the truth of it, he was
tempted to conſider the art of dancing
in thoſe times as ſomething wholly different from what is at preſent underſtood by dancing.

The chevalier Ramſay places it alſo
among the loſt arts.   Both, no doubt,
grounding their opinion on that deficiency of execution on the modern
theatres, compared to what is incon-
teſtably tranſmittedto us, by hiſtory, of
the excellence of the antient pantomimes.

But none have more contributed to
eſtabliſh the opinion of the pantomime
art being an art totally different from
that of dancing, and not merely an
improvement of it, as was certainly the
caſe, than ſome of the profeſſors of
the

the art themfelves, who even exclaimed
againſt M. Cahuſac, for his attempts
to give juſter notions, and to recommend the revival of it.

We are too apt to pronounce upon
poſſibilities from our own meaſure of
knowledge, or of capacity. Nothing is
more common than to hear men of a profeſſion declare loudly againſt any practice attempted to be eſtabliſhed for the
improvement of their art, and perempto-
rily to aver ſuch a practice being impoſſible, for no other reaſon than that
their own ſtudy and efforts had not
been able to procure them the attainment of it.   In this too they are ſe-
conded by that croud of ſuperficial people who frequent the theatres, and
who can believe nothing beyond what
themſelves have ſeen: any thing above
the reach of what they are accuſtomed

or

or habituated to admire, always feems to them a chimera.

The reproach of incredulity is commonly made to men of the greateft knowledge, becaufe they are not over-apt to admit any propofition without proof: but this reproach may, with more juftice, be ofteneft made to the ignorant, who generally reject, without difcuffion, every thing beyond their own narrow conception.

To thefe it may found more than ftrange; it may appear incredible, that on the theatre of Athens, the dance of the Eumenides, or Furies, had fo expreffive a character, as to ftrike the fpectators with irrefiftible terror. The Areopagus itfelf fhuddered with horror and affright; men grown old in the profeffion of arms, trembled; the
mul-

multitude ran out; women with child miſcarried; people imagined they ſaw in earneſt thoſe barbarous deities commiſſioned with the vengeance of heaven, purſue and puniſh the crimes of the earth.

This paſſage of hiſtory is furniſhed by the ſame authors, who tell us, that Sophocles was a genius; that nothing could withſtand the eloquence of Demoſthenes; that Themiſtocles was a hero; that Socrates was the wiſeſt of men; and it was in the time of the moſt famous of the *Greeks* that even upon thoſe highly privileged ſouls, in ſight of irreproachable witneſſes, the art of dancing produced ſuch great effects.

At Rome, in the beſt days of thisart, all the ſentiments which the dancers expreſſed, had each a character of truth,

fo

so great a power, such pathetic energy, that the multitude was more than once seen hurried away by the illusion, and mechanically to take part in the different emotions presented to them by the animated picture with which they were struck. In the representation of *Ajax in a frenzy*, the spectators took such violent impressions from the acting-dancer who represented him, that they perfectly broke out, into outcries; stripped, as it were, to fight, and actually came to blows among each other, as if they had caught their rage from what was passing on the theatre.

At another time they melted into tears at the tender affliction of Hecuba.

And upon whom were these lively impressions produced? Upon the co-

F f   tem-

temporaries of Mecenas, of Lucullus, Auguftus, Virgil, Pollio; upon men of the moft refined tafte, whofe criticifm was as fevere as their appro-bation honorable; who never fpared their cenfure nor their applaufe, where either was due. How, efpecially un-der the eyes of Horace, could any thing pafs the approbation of the public, unlefs under the feal of excellence in point of art and good tafte? Would Auguftus have declared himfelf the fpecial patron of a kind of entertainment that had been deficient as to probability and ge-nius? Would Mecenas, the protector of Virgil, and of all the fine arts, have been pleafed with a fight that was not a ftriking imitation of beautiful nature?

The proofs fhown of the perfection of dancing at Athens, and under the reign of Auguftus, being inconteftable, it it is plain that what now paffes for the art of dancing, is as yet only in its infancy. To difplay the arms gracefully, to preferve the equilibrium in the pofitions, to form fteps with a lightnefs of air; to unfold all the fprings of the body in harmony to the mufic, all thefe points, fufficient to what may be called private, or to affembly-dancing, are little more than the alphabet of the theatrical dances, or of pantomime execution. The fteps and figures are but the letters and words of this art. A writing-mafter is one who teaches the mechanical part of forming letters. A mere dancing-mafter is an artift who teaches to form fteps. But the firft is not more different from what we call a man of letters, or a *writer*, than the fecond is from what may deferve on the theatre, the name of principal dancer.

Be-

Befides the neceffity of learning his art elementally, a dancer, like a writer, fhould have a ftile of his own, an original ftile: more or lefs valuable, according as he can exhibit, ex- prefs, and paint with elegance a great- er or leffer quantity of things admirable, agreeable, and ufeful.

Speech is fcarce more expreffive, than the geftual language. The art of painting, which places before our eyes the moft pathetic, or the moft gay images of human life, compofes them of nothing but of attitudes, of pofitions of the arms, expreffions of the counte- nance, and of all thefe parts dancing is compofed, as well as painting.

But, as I have before obferved, paint- ing can exprefs no more than an inftant of action. Theatrical dancing can exhibit

hibit all the fucceffive inftants it chufes to paint. Its march proceeds from picture to picture, to which, motion gives life. In painting, life is only imitated ; in dancing, it is always the reality itfelf.

Dancing is, evidently, in its nature, an action upon the theatres; nothing is wanting to it but meaning : it moves to the right, to the left; it retrogrades, it advances, it forms fteps, it delineates figures. There is only wanting to all this an arrangement of the motions, to furnifh to the eye a theatrical action upon any fubject whatever.

The hiftory of the art proves that the dancers of genius, had no other means or affiftance in the world but this to exprefs all the human paffions, and the

poffibilities

poſſibilities of it are in all times, the very ſame.

Both here, and in France, there have been ſome of theſe dramatic pieces in action, by dance, attempted, which have been well received by the public.

Some years ago, the Dutcheſs of Maine ordered ſimphonies to be compoſed for the ſcene of the fourth act of the *Horatii*; in which the young Horatius kills Camilla. Two dancers, one of each ſex, repreſented this action at *Sceaux*; and their dance painted it with all the energy and pathos of which it was ſuſceptible.

In Italy eſpecially many ſubjects of a what may be called low comedy, are very naturally expreſſed by dancing. In ſhort, there is hardly any comic action but what

what they reprefent upon their theatres, if not with perfection, at leaft fatis-factorily. And certainly the dance in action has the fame fuperiority over fheer unmeaning dancing, that a fine hiftory-piece has over cutting flowers in paper. In the laft there is little more required than mechanical nicety, and, at the beft, it affords no great pre-tention to merit. But it is only for genius to order, diftribute and compofe, in the other. A Raphael is allowed to take place in the Temple of Fame, by a Virgil ; and the art of dancing is ca-pable of having its Raphaels too. Pila-des, and Bathillus were painters, and great ones, in their way. Picturefque compofition is not lefs the duty of a compofer of dances, than of a pain-ter.

Among

Among the antients, that *Protheus*, of whom fabulous hiſtory records ſuch wonders, was only one of their dancers, who, by the rapidity of his ſteps, by the ſtrength of his expreſſion, and by the employment of the theatrical deceptions, ſeemed at every inſtant, to change his form. The celebrated *Empuſa* was a female dancer, whoſe agility was ſo prodigious that ſhe appeared and vaniſhed like a ſpirit.

But it was at Rome that the Pantomime art received its higheſt improvement. Pilades born in Cilicia, and Bathillus of Alexandria, where the two moſt ſurpriſing geniuſes, who, under the reigns of Auguſtus Cæſar, diſplayed their talents in their utmoſt luſtre. The firſt invented the ſolemn, grave and pathetic dances. The compoſitions of Bathillus

thillus were in the lively, gay, and fprightly ftile.

Bathillus had been the flave of Mecenas, who had given him his freedom in favor of his talents. Having feen Pilades in Cilicia, he engaged him to come to Rome, where he had difpofed Mecenas in his favor, who, becoming the declared protector of both, procured to them the encouragement of the Emperor.

A theatre was built for them: the Romans flocked to it, and faw, with furprife, a complete tragedy; all the paffions painted with the moft vigorous ftrokes of reprefentation: the expofition, plot, cataftrophe expreffed in the cleareft and moft pathetic manner, without any other means or affiftence but that of dancing, executed to the fimphonies

G g   the

the best adapted, and far superior to any that had been before heard in Rome.

Their surprise was not to end here. To this a second entertainment succeeded; in which an ingenious action, without needing the voice or speech, presented all the characters, all the pleasant strokes, and humorous pictures of a good comedy.

And in both these kinds, the executive talents of Pilades and Bathillus corresponded to the boldness and beauty of the kind of compositions they had ventured to bring on the stage.

Pilades especially, who was at the head of this project, was the most singular man that had till then appeared on the theatre. His fertile imagination

tion conftantly fupplied him with new means of perfecting his art and embel-lifhing his entertainments. Athenæus mentions his having written a book much efteemed on the depths and principles of his art.

· Before him, fome flutes compofed the orcheftra of the Romans. He re-inforced it with all the known inftru-ments. He added chorufes of dances to his reprefentations, and took care that their fteps and figures, fhould al-ways have fome relation or affinity to' the principal action. He provided them with dreffes in the higheft tafte· of propriety, and omitted nothing towards producing, keeping up, and pufhing to the higheft pitch, the charm of the theatrical illufion.

The actions on the Roman theatres were tragic, comic, or satirical; thefe laft pretty nearly anfwering to what we underftand by grotefque or farcical.

Efopus and Rofcius had been, from their excellence in declamation, the delight and admiration of Rome. But on their leaving no fucceffors to their degree of merit; the tafte for dramatic poetry which was no longer fupported by actors equal to them, began to decline; and the theatrical dances under fuch great mafters as Pilades and Bathillus, either by their novelty, or by their merit, or by both, made the Romans the lefs feel their lofs of thofe incomparable actors. The geftual language took place of that which was declaimed; and produced regular pieces acted in the three kinds of tragedy, comedy, and farce or grotefque. The

fpectators

fpectators grew pleafed with fuch an exercife of their underftanding. Steps, motions, attitudes, figures, pofitions, now were fubftituted to fpeech; and there refulted from them an ex- preffion fo natural, images fo re- fembling, a pathos fo moving, or a pleafantry fo agreeable, that people ima- gined they heard the actions they faw. The geftures alone fupplied the place of the fweetnefs of the voice, of the energy of fpeech, and of the charms of poetry.*

This

---

*Hanc partem Muficæ difciplinæ Majores mutam nominârunt, quæ ore claufo loqui- tur, et quibufdam gefticulationibus facit intelligi, quod vix narrante lingua, aut fcripturæ textu poffit agnofci.

Caffiod, var. 1. 20.

Loquaciffimas manus, linguofos digitos, filentium clamofum, expofitionem tacitam.

Idem.

This kind of entertainment, so new, though formed upon a ground-work already known, planned and executed by genius, and adoped with a passionate fondness by the Romans, was called the *Italic dance*; and in the transports of pleasures it caused them, they gave to the actors of it, the title of *Pantomimes*. This was no more than a lively, and not at all exagerated expression, of the truth of their action, which was one continual picture to the eyes of the spectators. Their motion, their feet, their hands, their arms, were but so many different parts of the picture; none of them were to remain idle; but all, with propriety, were to concur to the formation of that assemblage, from which result the harmony, and, with pardon for the expression, the happy *all-together* of the composition and performance. A dancer learned from his

very

very name of *pantomime*, that he could be in no efteem in Rome, but fo far as he fhould be *all the actor*.

And, in fact, this art was carried to a point of perfection hard to believe; but for fuch a number of concurrent and authentic teftimonies.

It appears alfo clearly from hiftory, that this art, in its origin, (fo favored by an arbitrary prince, and who alfo made fome ufe of it, towards eftablifh- ing his defpotifm, nay even primordi- ally introduced by Bathillus, a flave) could no longer preferve its great ex- cellence, than the fpirit of liberty was not wholly worn out in the Roman breafts; and, like its other fifter arts, gradually decayed and funk under the fubfequent emperors.

Pilades

Pilades gave a memorable inftance of the (as yet) unextinguifhed fpirit of liberty, when, upon his being banifhed Rome, for fome time, by Auguftus Cefar, upon account of the difturbances the pantomime parties occafioned, he told him plainly to his face, that he was ungrateful for the good his power received, by the diverfion to the Romans from more ferious thoughts on the lofs of their liberty. "Why do "not you," fays he, "let the people "amufe themfelves with our quarrels?"

This dancer had fuch great powers in all his tragedies, that he could draw tears from even thofe of the fpecta-tors the leaft ufed to the melting mood.

But in truth, the effect of thefe pantomimes, in general, was prodigious.

Tears

Tears and fobs interrupted often the reprefentation of the tragedy of *Glaucus*,
in which the pantomime Plancus played
the principal character.

Bathillus, in painting the amours
of Leda, never failed of exciting
the utmoft fenfibility in the Roman
ladies.

But what is more furprifing yet,
Memphir, a Pithagorean philofopher,
as Athenæus tells us, expreffed, by
dancing, all the excellence of the phi-
lofophy of Pithagoras, with more elegance, more clearnefs and energy, than
the moft eloquent profeffor of philofo-
phy could have done.

Upon confidering all this, one is almoft tempted to fay, with M. Cahufac, " We have, upon the ftage, ex-
               H h   cellent

" cellent feet, lively legs, admirable
" arms : what a pity it is, that with
" all this we have fo little of the art of
" dancing!"

Our tragedy and our comedy have an
extent and duration which are fupported by the charms of fpeech, by the in-
tereftingnefs of narration, by the variety of the fallies of wit. The action
is divided into acts, each act into fcenes,
thefe fcenes fucceffively prefent new
fituations, and thefe fituations keep up
the warmth of intereft and attention,
form the plot, lead to the conclufion
or unravelment, and prepare it.

Such muft have been, or fuch muft
be, (but with more precifion and mark-
ingnefs) tragedies or comedies reprefented by dancing; as gefture is fomething more marking and fuccinct than
fpeech.

fpeech. There are required many words to exprefs a thought, but one fingle motion may paint feveral thoughts, and fituations.

In fuch compofitions, then, made to be danced, the theatrical action muft go forward with the utmoft rapidity : there muft not be one unmeaning entry, figure, or ftep in them. Such a piece ought to be a clofe crouded abftract of fome excellent written dramatic piece.

Dancing, like painting, can only prefent fituations to the eye; and every truly theatrical fituation is nothing but a living picture.

If a compofer of dances fhould undertake to reprefent upon the ftage any great action or theatrical fubject, he

H h 2 muft

muft begin by making an extract from it, of all the moft picturefque fituations. No other parts befide thefe can enter into his plan ; all the others are defect-ive or ufelefs, they can only embarras, perplex, confound, and render it cold and infipid.

Whereas, if the fituations fucceed one another naturally, and in great number ; if their being well linked to-gether conducts them with rapidity, from the firft fituation to the laft, which muft clearly and ftrikingly unravel the whole ; the choice is complete, and the theatrical effect will be fure.

It is that final effect, of which, in the execution, the compofer and performer muft never lofe fight. Succeffive pictures muft be exhibited, and ani-mated with all the expreffion that can

refult

refult from the impaffioned motions of the dance.

This was doubtlefs the great fecret of the art of Pilades, who fo highly excelled in his ideas of theatrical ex-preffion : this is, perhaps, too for all kinds of theatrical compofition, whe-ther to be declaimed, or to be executed by dancing, a general rule that is not to be flighted.

One inftance of the regard fhewn by Pilades to theatrical propriety is pre-ferved to us, and not unworthy of at-tention. He had been publickly chal-lenged by Hilas, once a pupil of his, to reprefent the greatnefs of Agamemnon : Hilas came upon the ftage with buf-kins, which, in the nature of ftilts, made him of an artificial height ; in con fequence of which he greatly over-
topped

topped the croud of actors who furrounded him. This paffed well enough,
'till Pilades appeared with an air, ftern
and majeftic. His ferious fteps, his
arms a-crofs, his motion fometimes
flow, fometimes animated, with paufes
full of meaning, his looks now fixed on
the ground, now lifted to heaven, with
all the attitudes of profound penfivenefs,
painted ftrongly a man taken up with
great things, which he was meditat-
ing, weighing, and comparing, with
all the dignity of kingly importance.
The fpectators, ftruck with the juftnefs,
with the energy and real elevation of fo
expreffive a portraiture, unanimoufly
adjudged the preference to Pilades,
who, coolly turning to Hilas, faid to him,
" Young man, we had to reprefent a king
" who commanded over twenty kings : you
" made him tall: I fhowed him great."

It

It was in the reign of Nero, that a cinical mock-philofopher, called Demetrius, faw, for the firft time, one of thefe pantomime compofitions. Struck with the truth of the reprefen-tation, he could not help expreffing the greateft marks of aftonifhment : but whether his pride made him feel a fort of fhame for the admiration he had involuntarily fhewn, or whether natu-rally envious and felfifh, he could not bear the cruel pain of being forced to approve any thing but his own fingula-rities ; he attributed to the mufic the ftrong impreffion that has been made upon him : as, in that reign, a falfe philo-fophy very naturally had a greater influ-ence than the real, this man was, it feems, of confequence enough for the managers of the dances to take notice of this partiality, or at leaft to be piqued enough, for their own honor, to

lay

lay a fcheme for undeceiving him. He
was once more brought to their theatre,
and feated in a confpicuous part of the
houfe, without his having been acquainted with their intention.

The orcheftra began : an actor opens
the fcene : on the moment of his en-
trance, the fimphony ceafes, and the
reprefentation continues. Without any
aid but that of the fteps, the pofitions
of the body, the movements of the
arms, the piece is performed, in which
are fucceffively reprefented the amours
of Mars and Venus, the Sun difcover-
ing them to the jealous hufband of the
goddefs, the fnares which he fets for
his faithlefs fpoufe and her formidable
gallant, the quick effect of the trea-
cherous net, which, while it com-
pleats the revenge of Vulcan, only pub-
lifhes his fhame, the confufion of Venus,

nus, the rage of Mars, the arch mirth of the gods, who came to enjoy the fight.

The whole audience gave to the excellence of the performance its due applaufe, but the Cinic, out of himfelf, could not help crying out, in a tranfport of delight ; " *No ! this is not a reprefen-* " *tation ; it is the very thing itfelf.*"

Much about the fame time a dancer reprefented the *labors of* Hercules. He retraced in fo true a manner all the different fituations of that hero, that a king of Pontus, then at Rome, and who had never feen fuch a fight before, eafily followed the thread of the action, and charmed with it, afked with great earneftnefs of the emperor, that he would let him have with him that extraordinary dancer, who had made

I i   fuch

such an impreſſion upon him. "Do
" not, ſays he to Nero, be ſurpriſed at
" my requeſt. I have for borderers
" upon my kingdom, ſome Barbarian
" nations whoſe language none of my
" people could underſtand, nor they
" learn ours. Such a man as this
" dancer would be an admirable in-
" terpreter between us."

It would then ſurely be a great error
to imagine, that an habitual dexterity,
a daily practice, with their arms, their
legs and feet, were the only talents
of theſe pantomime dancers. Their
execution, without doubt, required all
theſe advantages of the body in the moſt
eminent degree ; but their compoſitions
ſuppoſed, and indiſpenſably implied
an infinite number of combinations
which belong intirely to the mind,
or intellectual faculties ; as for example,
                                        eſpe-

efpecially an attentive and judicious dif-
cernment of the moft interefting truths
of human nature. How extenfive a
ftudy this exacts, it is more eafy to
conceive than to attain.

And furely there is an evident neceffity for ftudying men, before one can
undertake to paint or reprefent them.
It is not till after a profound examination of the paffions, that one ought to
flatter one's felf with characterifing
them purely by the powers of external
figns of actions. All the paffions
have affinities to each other, which it
is only for a great juftnefs of underftanding to feize ; they have fhades
that diftinguifh them, which nothing
but a nice eye can perceive, and which
eafily efcape a fuperficial obferver.

In

In ſerious dancing, where the cha-
raƈter of a hero is to be given, there
are in his aƈtions, in the courſe of his
life, certain marking ſtrokes, certain in-
cidents or extraordinary paſſages, which
are ſubjeƈts proper for the ſtage, and
which muſt be ſeparated from others
perhaps more brilliant in hiſtory, but
which would infrigidate a theatrical
compoſition.

In the ſtate of dancing of our days,
the dancers, and even the compoſers of
dances, aſpire to little more than the
mechanical part of their art; and, indeed, they hardly know any thing beyond that, and cannot in courſe, cultivate what they have no conception.
of.

When M. Cahuſac wrote, he obſerved that this was ſufficient for the
ſpeƈtators

spectators, who required nothing more than a brilliant execution from the dancers in the old track of steps and capers; and this is, in fact, true of the greater number now. But lately, the taste for dances of action, animated with meaning and conveying the idea of some fable or subject, has begun to gain ground. People are less tired with a dance, in which the understanding is exercised, without the fatigue of perplexity, than by merely seeing a succession of lively steps, and cabriols, however well executed; which, in point of merit, bear no more proportion to that of a well-composed dance, than a tiresome repetition of vignettes, of head-pieces and tail-pieces, would do to the gravings of historical pieces after a Raphael, a Michael Angelo, or a Correggio.

As

As hitherto the compofer of the dances of action, have not been able to recover that height of perfection to which the antient pantomimes carried their art ; the moft that any compofers could do, I mean with fuccefs, (for there have been fome attempts made, that, for want of a proper plan and execution, failed,) was to furnifh certain dances, in the nature of *poemetti* or fmall dramatic poems, which, where the fubject of action has been clearly and intelligibly executed, have ever been received with the moft encouraging applaufe by the public.

And here the ingenious author to whom I am fo much obliged in this chapter, furnifhes me with rules of compofition for the dances of action, which can hardly be too much recommended.

All

All theatrical compofitions ought to have three effential parts.

By a lively dialogue, in a piece made to be fpoken, or by an incident dextroufly introduced in one made for a dance in action, the fpectator is to be prepared for the fubject that is to be reprefented, and to have fome acquaintance of the character, quality, and manners of the perfons of the drama: this is what is called *the expofition.*

The circumftances, the obftacles which arife our of the ground-work of the fubject, embroil it, and retard its march without ftopping it. A fort of embarrafment forms itfelf out of the actions of the characters, which perplexes the curiofity of the fpectators, from whofe even guefs-work, the manner how all is to be ultimately unravelled is

to

to be kept as great a fecret as poffible :
and this embarrafment is what is called *the plot*.

From this embarrafment, one fees
fucceffively   break   forth   lights,   the
more unexpected, the better.   They
unfold the action, and conduct it by
infenfible degrees to an ingenious conclufion : this is what is called *the unravelment*.

If any of thefe three parts is defect-
ive, the, theatrical merit is imperfect.
If they are all three in due proportion,
the action is complete, and the charm
of the reprefentation is infallible.

As the theatrical dance then is a reprefentation, it muft be formed of thefe
three effentially conftitutive parts. Thus
it will be more or lefs perfect, according

ing as its expofition fhall be more or lefs
clear, its plot more or lefs ingenious, its unravelment more or lefs ftriking.

But this divifion is not the only one
that fhould be known and practifed.
A dramatic work is commonly compofed of five or fewer acts; and an act
is compofed of fcenes in dialogue or
foliloquy. Now every act, every fcene,
fhould have, fubordinately, its expofition, its plot, and its unravelment,
juft as the total of the piece has, of
which they are the parts.

So ought alfo every reprefentation in
dancing to have thofe three parts, which
conftitute every thing that is action.
Without their union, there is no action
that is perfect : a fault in one of thofe
parts will have a bad effect on the
K k   others;

others ; the chain is broke ; the picture, whatever beauty it may have in other respects, is without any theatrical merit.

Besides these general laws of the theatre, which are in common to those compositions of dances, that are to be executed on it, they are subjected to other particular rules, which are derived from the primitive principles of the art.

As the art of dancing essentially consists in painting by gestures and attitudes, there is nothing of what would be rejected by a painter of good taste, that the dancer can admit; and, consequentially, every thing that such a painter would chuse, ought to be laid hold of, distributed, and properly placed in a dance of action.

Here

Here, on this point, recurs that never too often repeated rule, as infallible as it is plain : *let nature, in every thing, be the guide of art ; and let art, in every thing, aim at imitating nature :* a rule this, than which there is not one more trite, more hackneyed in the theory, nor leſs regarded in the practice.

Nature then being always Nature, always invariable in her operations and productions ; there is no falſe concluſion, nor ſtraining inferences, in avering, that the art of dancing could not but be a great gainer by a revival of the taſte of the antients for the pantomime branch ; which, upon the theatre, converted a tranſient flaſhy amuſement of the eye, into a rational or ſenſible entertainment, and made of dancers, who are otherwiſe, a mere mechani-

K k 2 cal

cal compofition of feet, legs, and arms,
without fpirit or meaning, artifts formed to paint with the moft pathetic expreffion, the moft ftriking fituations of
human nature: I am not afraid of ufing
here the term of the moft pathetic expreffion, injurioufly to the great power
of theatrical declamation ; becaufe the
great effect and charm of the moment is, evidently, the more likely
to be produced by attitudes or geftures
alone, unfeconded by the voice; for that
the pleafure of the fpectator will have
been the greater for the quicknefs
of his apprehenfion not having needed
that help to underftand the meaning of
them. And this is fo true of the force
of impreffion depending on that part
of bodily eloquence, that even in ora-
tory, action was, by one of the greateft judges of that art, pronounced to
be the moft effential part of it.

This

This may be, perhaps, an exaggeration : but when people refort to a theatre to unbend, or relax, they will hardly think their pleafure taftelefly diverfified by a fine pantomime execution of a dramatic compofition, to the perfection of which, poetry, mufic, painting, decoration, and machinery will have all contributed their refpective contingents.

For the fubjects of thefe poetical dances, the compofer will undoubtedly find thofe which are the moft likely to pleafe, in fabulous hiftory, efpecially for the ferious, or pathetic ftile. This we find was the great refource of the antients, who had, in that point, a confiderable advantage, from which the moderns are excluded, by the antient mithology having loft that effect, and warmth of intereft, which accomcompanied all tranfactions taken from it by their poets, and brought upon the theatre. The heroes of antiquity, the marvellous of their deities, and the hiftories of their amours, or of their exploits, can never make the fame impreffion on the moderns fo thoroughly differing in manners and ways of thinking, from thofe, to whom fuch exhibitions were a kind of domeftic, and even religious remembrancers. The fpectators of thofe times were more at home to what they faw reprefented upon their theatres; the ground-work of the fable reprefented to the audience being generally foreknown, contributed greatly to the quicknefs of their apprehenfion; and its being part of their received theology, and often of the hiftory of their own country, procured it the more favorable attention.

The

The greateſt part of theſe advantages are wanting in the employment of theſe fictions among the moderns; and to which however they are, in ſome meaſure, compelled to have recourſe, for want of theatrical ſubjects ſtriking enough to be agreeably thrown into a dance; by which I do not mean to exclude all ſubjects that have not thoſe poetical fictions of Greek and Roman antiquity for a baſis; on the contrary, it might juſtly paſs for a barrenneſs of invention, the being reduced conſtantly to borrow from them, but purely to point out a treaſure, ever open to the artiſt who ſhall know how to make a ſelection with judgment and taſte: always remembering, that the more univerſally the fable is foreknown, the more eaſy will the taſk be of rendering it intelligible in the execution.

There

There are, doubtlefs, fome parts of the antient mithology fo obfcure, and fo little known, that any plan taken from them, would, to the generality of the fpectators, be as great a novelty, as if the compofer had himfelf invented the fubject. There are others again of which all the intereft is entirely antiquated and exploded.

As to the pieces of compofition in the comic vein, there is nothing like taking the fubject of them from the moft agreeable and the moft marking occurrences in real, current life; and the ftronger they are of the manners and practice of the times, the nearer they will feem to the truth of nature, and the furer at once to be underftood, and to have a pleafing effect.

And

And here I shall take the liberty of concluding with offering two instances of poetic dances; the one in the serious, the other in the comic vein, which are furnished rather as hints of the improvable nature of such compositions, than in the least meant for models of them.

The first has for title,

VENUS and ADONIS.

The decoration represents a wood interfected by several walks, which form an agreeable perspective of distances. At the bottom of the theatre, and in the middle, there is a grand walk, terminated by a small mount, on the summit of which is seen a colonnade, that forms the peristile of a temple.

L l   Venus,

Venus, preceded by the Graces and several nimphs, comes out of the temple, descends the mount, and advances to the front of the wood; the simphony to be the most agreeable and melodious imaginable, to announce the arrival of the goddefs of love.

The Graces and the nimphs open the action, and by their gestures and steps, exprefs their endeavour to sooth the impatience of Venus on the absence of Adonis. The agitation in which she is, ought to be painted on her countenance, and expressed by the discompofure of her steps, marking her anxiety and defire of feeing her lover.

The found of the chace is heard, which betokens the approach of Adonis. Joy breaks forth in the eyes, the gestures, and steps of Venus and her train.

Adonis,

Adonis, followed by feveral hunters, enters through one of the fide-walks of the wood. Venus runs to meet him, and feems to chide him for having been fo long away. He fhows her the head of a ftag, which he has killed, and which is carried, as in triumph, upon a hunting-pole, by one of the hunters; and offers it, as the fruit of his chace, in homage to the goddefs, who is prefently appeafed, and gracioufly receives his offering. Thefe two lovers then exprefs in a *pas-de-deux*, their mutual fatisfaction.

The hunters mix with the Graces and nimphs, and form a dance which characterifes their harmony.

Soon a noify fimphony, of military inftrumental mufic, gives warning of the arrival of Mars. Venus, Adonis,

the

the Graces, the nimphs, and hunters, show signs of uneasiness and terror.

Mars, followed by several warriors, enters precipitately through a walk opposite to that by which Adonis and the hunters came. Venus separates from Adonis, having insisted on his getting out of the way of the formidable god of war. He withdraws with his train by the same way as he came. Mars, inraged with jealousy, makes a shew of going to pursue Adonis. Venus stops him, and employs, in her soothing and caresses, all the usual arts of appeasing and blinding a jealous lover. She prevails at length, not only to dissipate his passion, but to make him believe himself in the wrong for having been jealous.

The

The warriors addrefs themfelves to the Graces and nimphs, and form together a dance expreffive of a fort of reconciliation ; after which Mars and his train return by the fame way as they came.

Venus, the Graces, and the nimphs, fee them go, and when they are got a little diftance from them, teftify their fatisfaction at having got fo well over this interruption.

Adonis returns alone : Venus fprings to meet him, and gives him to underftand that he has now nothing to fear ; that Mars will not return in hafte.

In the fame walk from which Adonis came, the hunters of his train are feen purfuing a wild boar, that tries to efcape juft by where the Graces and the nimphs are,

278 A TREATISE ON THE

are, who, in their fright, attempt to
fly from him : but he is already fo near
them, that they do not know how to
avoid him. Adonis runs haftily to pierce
the boar with his javelin; but the boar
gets him himfelf down. The hunters
arrive at that inftant, and kill the boar;
but Adonis is neverthelefs mortally
wounded, and expires.

Here it is that the mufic and the
dance are to difplay their refpective
powers : the one by the moft plain-
tive mournful founds; the other by
geftures and fteps in which grief and
defpair are ftrongly characterifed, ought
to exprefs the profound affection into
which Venus is plunged, and the fhare
the Graces, the nimphs, and the hunters take in it.

Venus

Venus appears to implore the aid of all the gods, to reftore her lover to her. She bathes him with her tears, and thofe precious tears have fuch a virtue, that Adonis appears all of a fudden transformed into an anemony or wind-flower.

The Graces and the nimphs exprefs their furprife; but the aftonifhment of the hunters fhould be yet more ftrongly marked.

Venus herfelf is not the more com-forted by this metamorphofis. A flower cannot well fupply the place of her lover. She turns then her eyes to-wards the earth, and feems to invoke the power of fome deity inhabitant of its bowels.

The

The flower difappears; the earth opens, and Proferpine rifes out of it, fitting on a chariot drawn by black horfes, and having at her fide Adonis reftored to life.

It is natural to imagine the joy that is at this to be expreffed, by the fimphony, by the geftures, and fteps of of Venus, of the Graces, the nimphs, and hunters.

Proferpine, getting out of her chariot, holding Adonis by the hand, prefents him to Venus. A *pas-de-trois* or trio-dance follows, in which the joy of the two lovers at feeing one another again is to be characterifed by all the expreffion, and all the graces of the moft pleafing dance, while Proferpine teftifies her fatisfaction at having produced the re-union : after which, fhe

gets

gets into her chariot, and re-defcends into the earth.

The Graces, the nimphs, and hunters, exprefs how highly they are charmed at feeing Adonis again ; Venus and Adonis form a *pas-de-deux*, or duet-dance, in which the Goddefs takes off her girdle or *ceftus*, and puts it upon Adonis, in the way of a fhoulder-belt, or as now the ribbons of moft orders of knight-hood are worn, which is to him a fimbol of immortality.

The Graces and nimphs teftify to Adonis how pleafed they are to fee him received into the number of the demi-gods : the hunters pay their homage to him, and the whole concludes by a general country-dance.

M m   The

The other specimen has for title,

The Coquette Punished.

The decoration represents a delicious garden, in which there are several compartments, separated by canals and *jet-d'eaux*. This scenery should exhibit the prospect of at once a pleasure-garden, and a fruit-one.

In the bottom of this perspective, there appear several gardeners busied, some in pruning the hedges, others in sowing and planting : more towards the front are seen, some women at work, tying up the flowers, or cleaning them from pernicious leaves ; others setting roots in vases. All this forms the scenical picture at the drawing up the curtain.

A

A fimphony mixed with the moft rural inftruments of mufic, begins with foft and foothing airs.

One of the female gardeners, more fhowifhly dreffed than the others, and who is employed upon fome neceffary tafk about the flower-vafes, feems however more attentive to the admiring the flowers, than to do her work: and as fhe is ftanding near a canal, fhe is, when fhe imagines none are taking notice of her, looking at her figure in the watery mirror, admiring herfelf, and adjufting her drefs. Though fhe does all this by ftealth, her companions remark her coquettry, make figns to each other, and point her out to the gardeners, who join the laugh at her, without the coquet's perceiving it, who is too much taken up with herfelf.

The fimphony fhould exprefs by the founds, as nearly as poffible, the mockery and burfts of laughter from the reft of the gardeners.

The coquet is fadly tempted to gather fome of the flowers for her own ufe, but dares not. In the moment that fhe is expreffing the greateft mind for it, enters a gardener, who is not one of thofe employed at work, and who makes up to her, fhows her a fine nofegay, and fignifies to her that he is come on purpofe to offer it her. The coquet immediately leaves off her work; and this *pas-de-deux* begins by all the little grimaces and falfe coynefs that the coquette oppofes to her acceptance of the nofegay, but which at the fame time only the more betray the mind fhe has for it. The gardener keeps preffing her to receive it. Her companions, curious

curious to fee how this will end, advance little by little towards them:
the gardeners follow them; and all
furrounding the coquette and her fwain,
form a dance, in which the men feem
to excite the lover not to take a denial,
and the women want to engage the coquette to receive the nofegay ; but all
this, with a bantering air : at length
the coquette accepts it, fticks fome of
the flowers in her hair, and the reft in
her bofom. Her companions and the
gardeners, fhew by their figns, that
they were very fure fhe would take
the nofegay and return to their,
work.

Another gardener now enters, on
the fide oppofite to that on which
the firft came, and advancing with an
air of gaiety, prefents to the coquette, a
fmall bafket of fine fruit. In this *pas-
de-trois,*

de-trois, she a-fresh makes a great many faces, about whether she will take the fruit or not. The swain of the nosegay expresses his vexation at the intervention of this rival, but the co-quette manages so well that she pacifies his jealousy, and accepts the other's basket of fruit, which she hangs upon her arm. The gardeners do not quit their work, but they give to under-stand by shrewd signs, what they think of the coquette's game.

It is easy to conceive, that the com-poser of this music will, in the airs made for the *pas-de-deux,* and *pas-de-trois,* pay attention to the different affections that are to be characterised by the dance.

While the gardener who brought the nosegay, and the other who presented

fented the fruit, and the coquette, are all feemingly in good harmony, enters a third gardener, gallantly dreffed, of a moft engaging figure, having in his hands fome pink-and-filver ribbons.

The fimphony fhould announce the arrival of this amiable gardener, by an air all expreffive of brifknefs and gay gallantry.

The gallant gardener approaches the coquette, and fhews her thofe glittering ribbons, which at once catch her eye, and give her a violent longing for them. This new-comer takes notice of the flowers in her hair and bofom, and of the fruit-bafket hung upon her arm. He gives her plainly to underftand that fhe muft return all this to his rivals, if fhe has a mind to have the ribbons. Thefe

begin

begin to exprefs their refentment; but
the coquette is fo tranfported with the
pleafure of bedizening herfelf with thofe
ribbons, that no regard can with-hold
her: fhe returns the flowers to the
one, and the fruit to the other, and
takes the ribbons. The two gardeners,
who fee themfelves flighted in this
manner, threaten him who has given
the ribbons, and throw themfelves into
attitudes of falling upon him; at which
he puts on a refolute look, and does
not feem to fear them. Her companions and the gardeners leave their
work, and advance fome fteps forwards, being curious to fee how the
fcene will end.

The fimphony fhould here exprefs,
by different airs, the refentment of the

two

two firſt ſwains, and the reſentment of
the gallant gardener.

The coquette uſes her beſt arts to
pacify the two angry gardeners ; but it
is all in vain; they expreſs their indignation, and are determined to take their
revenge upon their rival: Juſt in the
inſtant, and they are preparing to
attack him, and that he is ſtoutly ſtand-
ing upon his defence, comes in a
female gardener, amiable, lively, but
without any mark of coquettry in her
looks or dreſs, who, by the eager and
frightened air with which ſhe inter-
poſes, and places herſelf between the
gallant gardener and the others, to
prevent their hurting him, diſcovers the
tender regard ſhe has for him.

N n   The

290 A TREATISE ON THE

The two others, in refpect to this charming girl, dare not proceed; but, they give her to underftand that the coquette has been fo bafe as to return the flowers to the one, and the fruit to the other, that fhe might get the ribbons from the gardener whom fhe is protecting from their juft refentment.

At this the offended fair one ex-preffes to her lover her indignation, but does not the lefs for that make the others fenfible that fhe will not fuffer them to hurt him. She fnatches next, from the coquette, the ribbons. The whole company round teftify their approbation of what fhe has done, even the two gardeners, who were, the moment before, fo angry, burft out a-laughing for joy, to fee the coquette fo well punifhed, being now left without flowers, fruit, or ribbons; at which

which she withdraws, overwhelmed with confusion, and with the loud laugh and rallying gestures of her companions and the other gardeners.

The gay gardener, vexed at having been surprised by his mistress, in an act of gallantry to another woman, wants to pass it off to her as merely a scheme to amuse himself, and to laugh at the coquette. At first she will. not hear him ; she treads the ribbons under her feet, and is going away in a passion. He stops her, and entreats her forgiveness with an air so moving and penetrated, that, little by little, she is disarmed of her anger, and pardons him, in sign of which she gives him her hand.

There is no need of specifying here what the dance in action, accompanied

by

by the mufic, fhould exprefs in this *pas-
de-deux* ; & is too obvious

The gardeners, men and women,
teftify their rejoicing at this reconciliation, and the dance becomes
general.

F I N I S.

www.ingramcontent.com/pod-product-compliance
Lightning Source LLC
Chambersburg PA
CBHW020511270326
41926CB00008B/829